G000244745

Llama Drama Ding Dong!

The *Headline* Book of Headlines

Compiled and edited by

TONY LOYNES

HEADLINE

Tony Loynes is the Publisher/Editor of the *UK Press Gazette*, the weekly newspaper for journalists. For the past two years he has judged the newspaper's monthly headline competition.

This Collection Copyright © 1995 Tony Loynes

The right of Tony Loynes to be identified as the
editor and compiler of the Work has been asserted by him in
accordance with the Copyright, Designs and Patents Act 1988.

First published in 1995 by
HEADLINE BOOK PUBLISHING

First published in paperback in 1995 by
HEADLINE BOOK PUBLISHING

10 9 8 7 6 5 4 3 2 1

All rights reserved. No part of this publication may be
reproduced, stored in a retrieval system, or transmitted,
in any form or by any means without the prior written
permission of the publisher, nor be otherwise circulated
in any form of binding or cover other than that in which
it is published and without a similar condition being
imposed on the subsequent purchaser.

ISBN 0 7472 5217 3

Typeset by Avon Dataset Ltd, Bidford-on-Avon, B50 4JH

Printed and bound in Great Britain by
Cox & Wyman Ltd, Reading, Berks

HEADLINE BOOK PUBLISHING
A division of Hodder Headline PLC
338 Euston Road,
London NW1 3BH

Contents

Introduction

It's only a few words, more often than not hastily assembled, but the headline is the axis around which everything in a newspaper revolves.

It's both the shop window and the beating heart of the newspaper. It can be short, shocking and punchy, or erudite, clever and ironical but whatever the devices employed by the headline writer one test sums up a good headline: does it attract you to read the story?

On the wall of the *Sun*'s editorial floor is a sign which says: 'News is anything which makes the reader say "Gee whiz".' For them boldness is everything.

This book offers plenty of bold, shocking and even outrageous headlines but it also shows that headline writing is a craft of great subtlety and gentle humour. This is a tribute to the skill of those men and women who every day are given a few words and a tiny space in which to excite the interest of millions of newspaper readers.

Our thanks to the hundreds of journalists who contribute headlines week in and week out to *UK Press Gazette*'s Headline of the Month competition which inspired this book and to Roger Wolens whose sponsorship of the competition has made it such an enduring success.

Offerings of notable headlines for the next Headlines anthology can be sent to: Tony Loynes, c/o The Nonfiction Department, Headline Book Publishing, 338 Euston Road, London NW1 3BH. Those whose entries are published will receive an advance copy of the next edition.

Tony Loynes
June 1995

1

Bombs and Bullets

'It's strange that men should take up crime when there are so many legal ways to be dishonest.'

Al Capone

Crime was once the staple diet of the newspaper. Now it rarely occupies the front pages unless the crime is either very big or it involves some celebrated person. The criminals have moved into the background, preferring to make their ill-gotten gains by less obvious means than via a shotgun and a stocking mask. The newspapers, similarly, have realised that they can be more profitable by not constantly highlighting the violence of the communities in which their readers live. When crime does rear its head, very often it is given a lighter treatment by the headline writers. For them, too, there is less smash and grab.

In a stunt more appropriate to a World War Two 'B' movie, escapers tunnelled out of Durham's maximum security E-Wing using a pet hamster with a length of string tied to its leg to measure the length of their tunnel. The escape was foiled when three prisoners decided to go early.

The *Daily Express* headlined the story:

The great hamster jail break

Women were apparently breaking out of a prison in Yorkshire – but only long enough to ply their trade as prostitutes. Some were earning £200 a time before slipping back into jail. The *Daily Mirror* called this:

Porridge oats

The *News of the World* interviewed gangster Reggie Kray, serving life for the murder of Jack 'The Hat' McVitie, over tea and biscuits at Maidstone prison. The biscuits gave the headline writer the chance for this opportunistic effort:

I Could Just Murder Another McVitie

☆

The subsequent death of Reggie's brother Ronnie was greeted by the newspapers more as a dramatic moment in a long-running soap opera than the end of one of criminal history's more notorious gangsters.

The *Daily Mirror* announced:

Ron but not forgotten

☆

The *Guardian* covered the lavish East End funeral with:

The gang's all here to pay last respects to Ron

☆

And the *Sun* observed Reggie's tears at the burial with:

Reggie Cry

☆

When a bogus beggar, who drove to his pitch in a £10,000 car, was arrested by police the *Western Daily Press* head-lined the story:

Farewell to Alms

☆

Cold-hearted crooks stole the nativity scene from a local hospital in Manchester. The *South Manchester Reporter* announced:

Crooks made away with the manger

☆

And on a similar theme, when fighting broke out by the local nativity display *Kent Today* headlined the story:

Affray in the Manger

☆

A drunken policeman took his car to the local Kwik-Fit depot for an MoT test. Noticing that he was worse for wear, the fitters reported him to the local police. When he drove away he was arrested for drink driving.

The *Sun* used the company's own slogan for its headline:

You can't get nicked quicker than by a Kwik-Fit fitter

☆

Looters in Uckfield used the flooding of the town centre to raid the local Lo-Cost store as goods floated out into the street. The *Sun* told its readers:

High Street looters wade in like plague of Lo-Costs

☆

Curry wars in south London led to massive discounts on meals as Indian restaurants battled each other for customers. It all turned to violence in the end and the *Woolwich and Charlton Mercury* told its readers about the:

Argy bhajee!

☆

The Rose of Tralee pageant is normally a dignified affair. But on this occasion a reveller climbed the town's 25ft monument, the Pikeman, stripped naked and urinated from it. Inevitably, perhaps this became, in the *Sun*:

The Hose of Tralee

☆

A man who appeared in court on possession of cannabis charges told magistrates he smoked it to help him sleep. The *Crawley News* headlined the story:

Dopey Comes To Aid Of Sleepy

☆

A drunken sailor bit a Wren's bottom during shore leave from HMS Invincible. The *Daily Express* told readers about the:

Sailor who went too much to stern

☆

When a lifeboatman appeared as number 57 on the court list, charged with drunken driving, his name gave the headline writer on the *Southern Daily Echo* a ready-made opportunity:

Heinze Campbell lands in the soup

☆

The long search for terrorist Carlos the Jackal finally ended in his arrest and the *Sun* headlined the story:

The day of the shackle

And when the paper tracked down a jockey involved in a horse-doping scandal to a pony stable it told readers:

The *Sun* finds needleman
in haystack

Suburban crime – the theft of gnomes, lawn-mowers, even fully grown hedges – was highlighted in the *Sunday Express* under the headline:

Breakdown in suburban
lawn order

This green-fingered crime remained a favourite story, with the *Daily Mirror* reporting that theft of plants accounted for almost one-quarter of stolen goods. It was, they said:

Daylight shrubbery

The motorist who drove along the M40 at 96 mph while using both hands to do up his tie, was given short shrift in *The Times* under the headline:

Knot Guilty

Former Mayor Jane Chitty had her dog stolen while she

was sitting in her car. *Kent Today* told readers of her misery at the loss of the family pet under the headline:

It's Mrs Chitty's fang pangs

☆

An unemployed motorist sadly without the required insurance, came to court after a crash to face the music. The *Evening Gazette* in Blackpool told the story under the headline:

Third party, ire and left!

☆

An undercover exercise in which the police staged a punch-up in order to test reaction time, went sadly awry because they failed to warn anyone it wasn't real. Have-a-go heroes stepped in to help and witnesses called up the local police station to report the mêlée. They were totally unaware of the exercise.

The *North-West Evening Mail* told the story under the headline:

The secret policeman's brawl

☆

A dawn visit by police to the home of Kevin Maxwell, son of the disgraced, dead newspaper tycoon, seemed to have been telegraphed to the press who were also there waiting. So reporters were able to witness the reception when the police knocked on the door. It was reported, bluntly, in the *Sun* headline:

P*** off or I'll call the police.
We are the police Mrs Maxwell.

☆

Sonia Sutcliffe, wife of the Yorkshire Ripper, sued the *News of the World* for libel and lost. After previously collecting some £330,000 in libel damages against the newspapers for their coverage of the Ripper saga, she now faced legal bills of some £300,000. The *Sun* told her gleefully:

Sonia Bike

☆

Customs officials in Southampton like to use telephones to hide drugs when training their sniffer dogs. Don't ask why because this wasn't explained in the article in *BT Today*. But the company did supply the officers with lots of old phones and the editor of their company newspaper with the story – which he cleverly headlined:

Nick nack pack of smack,
give a dog a phone . . .

☆

Yorkshire Coast Radio, like most local radio stations, is happy to carry information about fêtes being organised in its area. The station made an announcement to that effect in the *Scarborough Evening News* which was headlined imaginatively:

Your fête is our destiny

Marcia Clark, the tough prosecutor in the O J Simpson trial, was somewhat unkindly shown topless in the *News of the World* under the headline:

L A Raw!

Still in America, a decade of litigation between a top psychiatrist and an ardent feminist finally reached the courtroom. The *Guardian* chuckled at the story with the headline:

Shrink rap

Sir Paul Condon, the Metropolitan Police Commissioner, recently warned the force that is was possible to commit 'noble cause corruption' where officers strengthened evidence against suspects who they were convinced were guilty. At an unnamed police station the fear of thievery is so strong that every department labels its own milk. The force newspaper, *Police Review*, headlined its story about this:

Noble cows corruption

The heart-rending tale of a woman whose boyfriend was trying to kill her was told in the *Daily Mirror*. Not much doubt about it really:

The pizza was full of prawns, anchovies and horse dope. My lover was trying to poison me

☆

A fraud trial was stopped, if you can believe this, because the four prisoners complained they were still hungry after lunch. Apparently they only had two sausages each! The judge ordered the catering staff to explain themselves though most of us thought it was the judge who had taken leave of his senses. The *Daily Star* ran the story thus:

Stop the trial . . . I've only had two sausages . . . Justice not served

☆

A thief appeared in court charged with stealing £71 worth of condoms. He claimed that these were not to satisfy some heroic sexual performance – they were for propagation, not to avoid procreation. Apparently, placed at the bottom of a seed tray they helped retain moisture. This was neither here nor there for the magistrates but the *Guardian* liked the story and headlined it:

Green-fingered condom thief stretches court imagination

The bizarre dying wish of an eccentric widow was that the village where she lived should build a gallows. And she left £10,000 in her will to do it. The *Daily Star* said:

No noose will be bad news . . .

Technically speaking, Fred West was guilty of nothing since he never got to trial. When he killed himself in prison, though, he did so in part to escape that trial and, said some newspapers, to save his wife the ordeal too. The *News of the World* claimed that West killed himself as a birthday present to wife Rose and headlined the story:

Happy ret-urns!

The problems of the Marquess of Blandford made sporadic forays on to the front pages, the most amusing of which came when police were searching for him after he failed to obey a court order. Somewhat shamefacedly they finally tracked him down . . . to the flat next door. Blandford was hauled out screaming expletives. The *Guardian* told the story thus:

Heir turns blue as 'Keystone' cops discover the runaway marquess at flat next door

Try to say this quickly. The *Daily Express* carried a story about a drugs gang which was caught red-handed after using travel agents Thomas Cook in a money-laundering operation. It was suspicious staff at the travel agents who tipped off the police. The tongue-twisting headline was:

Thomas Cook's crack crooks

The American ASP expanding baton was to go on trial with the Avon and Somerset police force. The *Guardian* headlined this:

Telescopic truncheon extends long arm of the law

Canary breeders in Cannock were put on the alert after thieves swooped (well, what else?) on a top breeder's aviary and stole ten pairs of prize-winning birds. The *Chase Post* headlined its story:

Half finched

The notorious Yakuza – Japan's version of the Mafia – tried to improve their public image by stepping in to help after the Kobe earthquake. The *South China Morning Post* greeted this unusual act of generosity with the headline:

Goodfella-san

The news that a golf course had been built at a jail holding drug smugglers and sex offenders offended the *Daily Express* which headlined its story:

Golf course prisoners are swinging for their crime

A Northamptonshire benefice decided to look for its new rector by advertising in *Motoring Life*. Admittedly the job was in Silverstone but nevertheless it raised a few eyebrows in more conventional clerical circles. The *Times* headlined the story:

Rev counter

Asil Nadir's sudden fall stunned the City which, only months before, had rated his Polly Peck company highly. When he fled the country the *Sun* told readers:

Asil Asit off

☆

On arrival in Turkish Cyprus he was greeted like a homecoming hero and, for a while, gave interviews in which he pledged his return and promised shareholders in his distressed Polly Peck company a swift return to good fortune. The *Sunday Telegraph* said:

Prophet of profit finds honour at home

☆

In one of the more bizarre crimes, burglars who feared Beauty the Bull Terrier posted a letter soaked in glue through the letter-box of the house before raiding it . The *Daily Mirror* said:

Gang superglues guard dog's jaws

☆

The apocryphal headline 'Small war not many hurt' was coined to illustrate the little-islander mentality of the UK since losing the empire. Foreign news, never mind foreign wars, occupies very little space in many of our newspapers; which means that unless the war is a biggie we seldom hear about it. We have, of course, had one or two of our own in recent years.

By 20 April 1982, the Falklands conflict was hotting up and Mrs Thatcher called a war-cabinet meeting which rejected peace moves by Argentina. The *Sun* reported the rejection bluntly:

Stick It Up Your Junta

And later:

The Sun says Knickers to Argentina

On 1 May 1982, the *Sun* told its readers: 'The first missile to hit Galtieri's gauchos will come with love from the Sun.' Its headline was:

Up Yours Galtieri

And as hostilities began the *Sun* recorded the early skirmishes as it would a soccer match:

Britain 6 (South Georgia, two airstrips, three warplanes), Argentina 0

Days later on 3 May our navy torpedoed the Argentinian cruiser, *General Belgrano*. The *Sun* bellowed in its first edition:

Gotcha

In later editions as the death toll was reported, common sense and decency overcame the excitement and it changed the headline to:

Did 1200 Argies Drown?

On 29 May, after the capture of Goose Green and Darwin the *Sun* was jubilant:

Paras rout Argies to seize Darwin and Goose Green

Events during World War Two were reported in a much more circumspect manner. For many hours on the night of 12 May 1941, Government censors stopped newspapers printing anything but the German version of Rudolf Hess's flight to Scotland. Germany was claiming that Hess was dead. Finally the *Daily Express* announced:

Deputy-Fuehrer Gives Himself Up

Saddam Hussein attempted briefly to ingratiate himself with the region's Muslim faithful, particularly the Iranians, after the débâcle of the Gulf War. It was a tactic which most saw as cynical and which the *Observer* summed up over its report:

Butcher, Faker, mischief-maker

While on duty in the Gulf during the war, our servicemen had their pay CUT. The newspaper which proudly claimed to support 'our boys' was outraged. The *Sun* described the government as:

Desert Prats

The coverage in many newspapers of the Gulf War was widely accused of jingoism. The newspapers involved made no excuses for supporting the cause and while there were arguments that it was their job to report the war accurately, the Ministry of Defence was in no doubt that it was their job to help win it.

As usual at moments of heightened passion in this country, the *Sun* led from the front, pulling no punches, as its series of headlines during those few critical days shows.

After the captured fliers Adrian Nichol and John Peters were shown on Iraqi television apparently having been tortured . . .

Bastards of Baghdad

After Patriot missiles blew four Iraqi Scud missiles out of the sky . . .

Patriots 4 – Scuds 0

After Iraqi planes fled to Iran to avoid being shot down

Caught with his fliers down

And on Saddam Hussein's offer of a withdrawal from Kuwait while continuing the Scud missile assault on Saudi Arabia . . .

Saddam the sham

Bullet-dodging Kate Adie was branded a prima donna by ITN veteran Sandy Gall for her performance during a Gulf War press conference. Adie, alleged Gall, took it upon herself to answer questions on behalf of General Sir Peter de la Billière. Adie hails from Sunderland but this didn't stop the evening newspaper, the *Echo*, headlining the story:

The gall of war Kate, by TV Sandy

2

Entertainment

'You grow up the day you have your first real laugh – at yourself.'

Ethel Barrymore

It's hard to escape the conclusion that without Freddie Starr some newspapers would have been the poorer over the years.

His regular appearances in the headlines have usually been self-inflicted but such is the pulling power now of the name that almost any headline with Freddie Starr in it had an added piquancy.

It probably all started with this *Sun* story: 'Zany comic Freddie Starr put a live hamster in a sandwich and ATE it, model girl Lea La Salle claimed yesterday.' The headline was no less suspicious than it was bizarre.

Freddie Starr ate my hamster

That headline re-appeared in a variety of forms. When Freddie Starr's horse, Minnehoma, took the bookmakers to the cleaners and won him more than £300,000 in the Grand National, the *Sun* recycled its headline with:

Bookies 'Ate Freddie Starr

☆

Several years later, Starr was photographed on a beach with his new bride and apparent evidence of his excitement thrusting from his swimming trunks. The *Daily Star* swiftly capitalised:

Is that a hamster in your shorts or are you just glad to see me?

☆

Years later, when his gardener appeared in court over allegations of missing jewellery, the headlines were less, well, savoury.

The gardener made a series of bizarre allegations about the comedian which were later disproved. But they allowed the *Sun* to recall its coverage of the saga of MP David Mellor.

Mellor, you may recall, resigned after an affair with Antonia de Sancha in which toe-sucking was an apparently enjoyable part. And his departure was announced by the *Sun* with the headline: 'From a toe-job to no job.'

So the *Sun* proclaimed:

I gave Freddie Starr a hoe job

The *Daily Mirror* summed it up with:

I had a kitchen roll with Freddie

☆

And the *Daily Star* hauled out the expression more usually employed in relation to sprinter Linford Christie:

I ate Freddie Starr's lunchbox

☆

When TV comic Jim Davidson, famous for his 'Nick Nick' jokes, had his show axed after a series of brawls the *Sun* headlined the story:

Nick Nick is Sacked Sacked

☆

On a similar theme the police in Killingbeck were in trouble with the planning authorities when they failed to get planning permission for slapping up posters advertising a fly-on-the-wall documentary about their police station. The *Yorkshire Evening Post* told readers:

'The Nick' nick is nicked!

☆

After the BBC had apparently paid £1,500 to enlarge the breasts of a model for a programme in the Ruby Wax Show, the *Sun*, which had been running a campaign about wasteful spending at the Corporation, announced:

New Boobs on the Beeb

☆

Obsessed as the *Sun* is with breasts, it is hardly surprising that they figure large in its headlines. When it was claimed that Madonna had been given breast implants the paper capitalised upon this and the running gag in the TV series ' 'Allo 'Allo' with:

Madonna With the Big Boobies

☆

When magician Roy Lee accused his wife of having an affair with a sailor, the *Sun* headlined the story:

Magic's Gone Out of My Marriage

☆

In Birmingham, plans to erect a statue to its famous son, comedian Tony Hancock, reached halfway stage with the money finally raised and just planning approval remaining to be sorted. The *Birmingham Evening Mail* told readers:

Hancock's Half ours

☆

Carry On star Barbara Windsor's new toy-boy boyfriend caused some raised eyebrows and not a few laughs after the *Sun* headlined their picture of her rushing from her home to star in the pantomime *Aladdin*:

Must Dash, I've Got Aladdin Tonight

☆

If 1993 had been an *annus horribilis* for the Queen, there was little doubt which figure had caused the most annoyance on the showbiz front. The *South Oxfordshire Courier*, echoing the sentiments of many about that blobbulous TV character, screamed:

Annus Horriblobbus

☆

His part creator, the TV star Noel Edmonds, is famous for 'gunge-ing' guests – dowsing them in evil, green liquid. But he was less keen to have it done to himself and fled when *News of the World* editor Piers Morgan tried. The perhaps predictable *Sun* headline the next day was:

Noel Coward

☆

1993 had been a bad year for Oliver Reed, the hard-drinking, brawling film star whose antics got him into endless trouble. Writing in the *Mail on Sunday* as Christmas approached, Dilly Keane called for forgiveness for the star:

Raise a glass, for 'tis the season to be Olly

☆

It's not often that the *War Cry*, the newspaper of the Salvation Army, is quoted but they beat the rest when stories first emerged about a re-make of *Gone With The Wind*.

Scarlett Gets Her Second Wind

☆

'It's true what they say,' announced a breathless *South Wales Post* journalist, 'black men really can dance.' As for the rest of her night at the Cardiff disco, it's probably best left to the newspaper's headline over the story:

Afro dizzy act

☆

Leonard Nimoy, better known as Mr Spock of 'Star Trek', wrote a play about painter Van Gogh's time in the south of France. The *Western Morning News* told us the story of it under this headline:

An Ear in Provence

☆

The new 'Star Trek' film *Generations* was a little confusing, the *Bristol Journal* decided. The appearance of two Captain Kirks didn't help. Its review of the film was headlined:

Do too many Kirks
spoil the plot?

☆

Still with 'Star Trek', its creator Gene Roddenberry died leaving a request that his ashes should be sent into orbit from a US space shuttle. The *Sun* called him:

The Ash-Tronaut

☆

News that a permanent Shakespeare venue was being created in the Yorkshire wolds was greeted by the *Daily Telegraph* in a suitable theatrical form:

All the Wold's a stage for Bard's new manor home

☆

Actor and comedian Dudley Moore hasn't had the best of fortune with his marriages – a problem strangely common for funny men. When he announced his fourth marriage, the *Daily Telegraph* announced:

Moore the marrier

☆

The *Daily Telegraph* asked writer Henry Roth why it took him sixty years to publish his second novel. The grumbling response gave them their headline:

The gripes of Roth

Most top fashion models are alarmingly slim but the French fashion designer Hervé Leger produces couture for the thinnest of the thin. Trading upon the name of the French comic-strip character, the *Sunday Times Magazine* introduced us to this fashion for the emaciated thus:

Hervé's Adventures of Thin-Thin

☆

In a big year for comebacks, *The Flintstones* movie and the Voodoo Lounge tour of the Rolling Stones rock group were in the news. The *Scotsman* cleverly combined the two with the headline:

Yabbadaba-voodoo! It's the Stones, a modern old-age family

☆

Today's rock stars are beginning to get as dirty and smelly as the idols of their parents' generation. The sixties habit of trashing hotel rooms and making the hotel chambermaid's life a misery was making a comeback, The *Times* told us under the headline:

Suites smell of success

☆

TV sit-com star Anton Rodgers married someone twenty-five years his junior, imitating his screen role in 'May to December', and for the *Oxford Journal* there was only one way to present the story:

Wife Imitates Art

☆

Pop legend Gerry Marsden, he of Gerry and the Pacemakers, walked out of a show, we were told, because he hadn't been given a private loo at the theatre. The *Sun* rightly took the mick:

You'll Never Wee Alone

☆

The Times theatre critic was less than enchanted with *The Editing Process*, a new play about the publishing business. Its headline:

Deadlines, dead lines

☆

The film *Four Weddings and a Funeral* gave headline writers hours of fun. When its star Hugh Grant was alleged to have sworn at a fan in an unguarded moment, the *Sun* gave us:

Four letters and a film star

☆

Ageing balladeer and sex symbol Tom Jones whose bumping and grinding routines on stage have his middle-aged female fans in paroxysms of excitement, was profiled in the *Guardian*. The piece was headlined:

Erogenous Jones

☆

The film *The Road To Welville* was the story of Kelloggs cereal manufacturer, the 'monstrous' Dr Kellogg. The review of the film in the *Daily Mail* was headlined:

Was Kellogg a cereal killer?

☆

Australian soaps 'Home and Away' and 'Neighbours' have provided a fund of headlines for the newspapers. When soap star Craig McLachlan battled with his estranged wife Rachel Friend over possession of their beachfront home, it brought the *Sun* headline:

Home and a War

☆

The earnings of corporate bosses were in the headlines for most of the year but one pointed out in his defence that his income pales into insignificance alongside that of pop stars. The newspapers probed the claim and found that Elton John topped pop's big-pay chart with £18 million a year. It brought the possibly predictable *Sun* headline:

Pocket Man

☆

The cancellation of the Christmas panto at Basildon not only disappointed legions of local children but cost the jobs of the professional actors and actresses lined up for the run of *Snow White*. The theatrical profession's newspaper the *Stage* summed it all up with:

Hi Ho, Hi Ho, It's Out Of Work We Go!

Rowan Atkinson's foolhardy decision to join Jayne Torvill and Christopher Dean in an ice-dance stunt for Comic Relief's Red Nose Day was welcomed in the *Sun* with:

Torvill 'n' Bean

A little later Atkinson announced that he was bored with Mr Bean and he was going to scrap the character. *Today* called this:

The has Bean

The fall of the Berlin Wall ironically seems to have led to a rise in fascist-style pop groups in the former Iron Curtain countries. *The Times* wrote about this phenomenon and especially about one group call Laibach. And it headlined the story:

Laibach and think of Hitler

The death of J.I.M. Stewart, better known as Michael Innes, one of the classier crime writers of our time, brought a welter of adulatory obituaries – and rightly so. Headlining an obituary is a delicate task – you mustn't be disrespectful but you still want to catch the reader's attention. The *Herald*, Glasgow, came up with the perfect device:

Snobbery with violence

Playwright, author, actor – the talents of Alan Bennett are enormously diverse. When he released his diaries they rocketed to the top of the charts and even kept the Pope's book from the number one slot. This was heady success by any standard and *The Times* told us the story with the splendid headline:

God and Bennett

Late arrivals at Stratford upon Avon's Swan Theatre caused a deal of argument and bickering among the audience. The story, when it hit the *Solihull Times*, was neatly summed up thus:

Is this a nagger I see before me?

More theatrical problems in Stratford upon Avon when the leading man in the local drama group pulled out at the last minute with no replacement. Into the breach stepped female director Carol Robson. And into the headline in the *Stratford upon Avon Herald* came a flurry of sexual innuendo:

Leading man's late withdrawal leads to a sex change

☆

And in a review of a new play about Jane Austen, the *Coventry Evening Telegraph* came up with the headline:

Austen's Maestros

☆

The *East Kent Mercury* wrote a story about the manager of a Christian youth club in the area, called the Carpenters' Arms. He had once been in a band with rock star David Bowie and playing the rock music theme for all it was worth, they headlined the story:

He used to play with Bowie but now he's with The Carpenters

☆

Bernardo Bertolucci's epic film *Little Buddha* set in the Himalayas attracted strong critical acclaim even if it wasn't such a success at the box office. The *Yorkshire Miner* reviewed it with the headline:

Finger on the Bhutan

☆

The picture coverage of a hairdressing and beauty contest at the local college hit the desk of the editors at the *North-West Evening Mail* with an ominous thud. Photographs of local people's children sell newspapers but they are darned hard to headline with originality and without giving offence. Their clever solution was:

Putting on
hairs and faces.

☆

What is art? It's the perennial question raked over whenever something a bit unusual– like a pile of bricks or a dead sheep – appears in an art gallery. Jeff Koons made his name with kitsch-art, which is tasteless and even vulgar, but curiously popular with some people. The *Sunday Times* reviewed his work less than enthusiastically with the headline:

Kitsch and sink

☆

In Havering, Essex, they were teaching aspiring rock and roll stars how to wiggle, waggle and twang. The Havering Bands Project still had a few places left, announced the

Romford Recorder, under the inspired headline:

Rock enrol

The amply built Spanish diva Montserrat Caballé told the *Sunday Telegraph* that she intended to ignore her critics and carry on singing. There didn't seem to be much doubt which camp the *Sunday Telegraph* fell into given its headline:

It's not over till the fat lady stops

And still with opera, the Hyde Park concert by Luciano Pavarotti was hit by a rainstorm which soaked rich and poor, not to mention the famous and the royal. A bedraggled Princess Diana was pictured with Prince Charles meeting Pavarotti after the concert under a *Sun* headline:

Pavawetti

The musical works of Andrew Lloyd Webber were frequently panned by the critics but the man who was responsible for *Phantom of the Opera* and many more was loved by his fans. The were, said the *Guardian*:

The fan club of the opera

Today came up with a story about the problems at a ballet company where eight dancers were pregnant:

Ballet's faux pas de deux

☆

The extraordinary sight of a comedian reaching across and grabbing the left breast of *A Fish Called Wanda* star Jamie Lee Curtis during a Hollywood awards event, was one of those moments when a headline writer makes his name.

Jamie Lee Curtis looked stunned for a moment but obviously decided that a slap in the face – though thoroughly deserved – might have brought unwanted publicity to the event. Instead she grabbed the comedian John Lovitz by his family silver.

Some chose to concentrate on the comedian's bare-faced grab, others looked at Jamie Lee Curtis's response. Either way it was a big one for the headline writers.

The *Sun* announced it as:

Groper is grabbed by Jamie Lee Curlies

And later:

A fist clawed Wanda

☆

The *Daily Telegraph* carried the story and picture (the breast grab not the balls grab) under the more discreet but no less good headline:

A hand called Wander

The newspapers had earlier been full of stories about the politically correct way to hug – as demonstrated by the Green Party's Miriam Kennett. 'The Green way to hug' announced the *Daily Express*.

Under a photograph of comedian Lovitz being tugged by the groin the *Daily Mirror* headline read:

Are you sure this is the Green Party hug, Jamie?

Supermodel Kate Moss whose scrawny, emaciated looks captured the hearts of coutouriers everywhere, started to put on weight. Yes, big news. It was a sensation in the dailies. The *Daily Mirror* announced:

Strolling Moss gathers a stone

then spoiled it by adding: 'well, 10lb at least'.

Spike Milligan has been a law unto himself for so many years it's hard to recall him ever being predictable. So an interview with him requires an unpredictable headline. The

Daily Mirror chose to produce one of his mini-poems:

Behold, Behold the Lamb of God, as it leaps and hops . . . For very soon the Lamb of God will be the Lamb of Chops

☆

Believe it or not – it's your choice – apparently a delinquent raccoon started behaving much better after watching 'Coronation Street'. It's Bet Lynch that Dylan is particularly fond of. The *Daily Star* told us the story with the headline:

Raccoonation Street

☆

Still with 'Coronation Street', the *Sunday Mirror* revealed, if that isn't too dramatic a word, that several of the soap opera's current stars had appeared in it years ago playing other characters. They had been theatrically reincarnated. For instance, twenty years ago waiter Carlos proposed to Mavis Riley. Malcolm Hebden who played Carlos returned as salesman Norris Cole. The headline was:

Reincarnation Street

☆

The affair between Paula Yates, the wife of Bob Geldof, and Michael Hutchence, the lead singer with INXS, encouraged the *Sun* to dig out an old photograph in which Yates interviewed the singer and appeared to be glancing at what is now colloquially called his 'lunchbox'. Aussie Hutchence apparently complained in the interview that people were more interested in his trousers than his music. The *Sun* quoted Yates as saying, 'I'm not surprised looking at those. They look a little tight.' Its less than subtle headline on the story read:

Michael Crutch-ence

The affair between the two deepened and Yates left the family home for Hutchence and was pictured tugging him around the nightspots of London. The *Daily Mirror* carried the picture with the headline:

Puller Yates

Rock stars' affairs are meat and drink for the tabloids and when rock musician Mark Knopfler's marriage hit the rocks the *News of the World* was swift, if not visionary, with the obvious headline:

Rock Star Marriage in Dire Straits

Richard Madeley and Judy Finnigan – better known to morning television viewers as Richard and Judy –

announced that they were adding a prime-time television show to their hectic schedule. Given the exhausting pace of their lives, *Today* wondered how they managed to get out of bed in the morning . . . under the headline:

Finnigan's wake?

A preview of the 'French and Saunders Christmas Special' in *Time Out* explained that it would take the form of a series of parodies of major literary works like *Martin Chuzzlewit.* The headline:

Parody on, dudes

The *European*'s Elan section reviewed a book about horror which claimed that it was the movie genre best suited to providing 'a darkly satirical commentary on society's deep-seated anxieties'. Summing that lot up in a headline which might make someone want to read it was difficult, but not impossible:

Honey, I kidded the shrinks

Steven Spielberg directed it and Michael Crighton wrote it, and it promised to be one of the more compelling American TV series of the year. The *Scotsman* warned us to watch out for it under the headline:

Back to the suture

Director Norman Jewison's latest offering, *Only You*, didn't go down well with the cinema critic of the *Barnet Borough Times*. It was corny, she told readers. *The Times'* headline writer picked up the theme with:

Only you can make this world seem trite

It's unlikely but true – Dr Oliver Sacks combines his work as a top neurologist with the rather more banal role of thriller writer. The *Evening Standard* went to meet him and the ensuing profile was headlined:

The joys of Sacks

Cars became the hot item to dress up fashion shoots, with all the top models posing, for all the world like those rather sad demo girls draped over gleaming motor cars in the early days of the motor shows. The *Daily Telegraph* reported this trend under the headline:

Girls torque

Stephen Fry's disappearance after quitting his West End stage show had the hacks combing western Europe for him. Meanwhile back at home he was none too popular with his acting colleagues or with some others. The brewers Whitbread decided that they no longer had need of his services in the TV ads which featured Fry as a smooth bar-steward.

The *Daily Mirror* headlined the news:

They've axed the poor bar-steward

While the *Sun* told readers:

Silly bar steward faces axe

The *Daily Mirror* tracked the actor down to his French hideaway and claimed an exclusive under the headline:

French Fry

'Red Dwarf' star Craig Charles found himself in Wandsworth jail – he was later proved innocent of the charges against him – and wrote a series of poems to keep himself sane during the humiliating ordeal. The *News of the World* said:

Rhyme and punishment

The same newspaper told readers that 'Darling Buds of May' star Catherine Zeta Jones was shedding her girl-next-door image and talking about sex and men in what newspapers love to call a 'no holds barred' interview.

Introducing this new image they said:

Meet Catherine Man Eater Jones

☆

True or not, the *News of the World* announced that film star John Hurt was leaving the family home to save his marriage. The star of *Elephant Man* and many other films allegedly admitted that heavy drinking and long periods away on location were the problem. How this would be resolved by even longer periods away from home seems unclear but it headlined the story:

Elephant man packs his trunk
to save his marriage

☆

And another film star was in the news about the same time. Richard Gere, who was married to actress Cindy Crawford, was alleged to be having an affair with a model. This secret affair became less so when the *Daily Mail* revealed all under the headline:

Only here for the Gere

☆

It was always said that the nasty East German spy called Wolf, who featured in the John le Carré books, had been modelled on a real spy called Markus Wolfe who later stood trial in Dusseldorf on a charge of treason. Le Carré wrote a piece in the *Guardian* explaining that the truth was rather

more banal. The name came from his old lawn-mower.
The piece was headlined:

The lawn-mower
that came in
from the cold

☆

Want to keep fit? Well, you could watch those breakfast
TV exercise classes or alternatively you could take up
gardening. The *Mail on Sunday* told readers that a couple
of hours digging or weeding was the equivalent of fifteen
minutes exhausting workout with the likes of TV's Mr
Motivator. The paper said:

'Call Me Mr Rotavator'

☆

'EastEnders' star Gillian Taylforth and her lover Geoff
Knights seemed always to be appearing in court. On
one occasion Knights appeared to answer the charge of
punch-ing Taylforth on the nose. The *Daily Star* called
him:

Beast Ender

☆

Two stage hypnotists, a man and a woman, stared into
each others' eyes and fell in love. Well, that's how the
Daily Mirror told the story. Sadly they were both

married at the time and walked out on their respective partners, which gave the *Mirror* the headline:

Dirty trancing

☆

The news that actress Sharon Stone of *Basic Instinct* fame was being lined up for the part of Patsy in the American version of 'Absolutely Fabulous' didn't go down well with the British press. *Today* shrieked:

'Absolutely preposterous'

☆

Kenny Everett's inevitable death was treated, largely, with surprising taste by the tabloids. There were acres of praise for the comedian's talents and headlines which generally avoided the mawkish or the malign. The *Daily Mirror* used one of Everett's catchlines for its centre-spread:

The worst possible waste

☆

The *Guardian* looked at the world of the female impersonator and headlined the story:

The man who would be queen

☆

Those Hollywood stars get paid fortunes for acting and seldom know when to stop. Last year's Oscars ceremony became a weepie as they turned on the tear-ducts; none more so than Tom Hanks whose Oscar speeches are becoming legendary for their sentimentality. The *News of the World* could stand it no longer:

Tom Hanky

The one who had a right to spill a few tears was actress and model Liz Hurley who, perhaps, had been better known as Hugh Grant's girlfriend but who, nevertheless, didn't quite deserve the post-Oscars put down from Joan Rivers. The comedienne asked her unkindly: 'And who are you?' The *Daily Star* headlined this:

Liz who-ley

The *Forrest Gump* film which swept the Oscars led many of us to wonder whether the all-American hero of the past was now being replaced with the all-American halfwit. But Cosmo Landesman in the *Guardian* said this would be as daft as assuming all Brits identified with Mr Bean. The headline, nevertheless, said:

Dum dee dumb

Actress Demi Moore was everywhere for a while and the

Guardian asked readers: 'How much Moore can anybody take?' It examined her career under the headline:

The Demi monde

For a while everything he did was a glorious success. Kenneth Branagh had the press eating out of his hand and after one press conference to mark the production of *Much Ado About Nothing* the *Guardian* acknowledged the fact:

Branagh from heaven cry tuned-in hacks

The story may have been tongue-in-cheek but the *Guardian* claimed that rock music and religion were very close. Both revolved around deities, beliefs, devotion and, yes, moral codes. Its headline was:

I second that devotion

Beatles fans were invited to raid their lofts for mementos of the group and bring them along for free valuation at a Pop and Memorabilia Roadshow in Nottingham. The *Nottingham Evening Post* headlined the news:

Raiders of the loft hark back to past.

When a star-spangled gathering in London was held to encourage people to attend Brighton's May festival, *The Times* called it:

Pier pressure

In the art world, the *Independent* told us, romanticism and naked ladies were out. What was now in was 'self-deprecating humour'. Its headline on the story was:

Any colour you like as long as it's a joke

A tearful Elton John picked up an Oscar for his *Lion King* sound track and dedicated it to his grandmother who had recently died. 'She was the one who sat me down at the piano when I was three,' he said. The *Sun* headlined its coverage:

The granny awards

An industrial tribunal in Stratford heard how a stage technician was sacked for urinating onto the stage from a gantry above. The *Warwickshire County Standard* said it was a case of:

To pee, or not to pee . . .

A summer fashion feature in the *Sunday Telegraph* looked at the coolest material to wear on those occasions when the British weather became overbearing. Linen, said their experts, was the answer for summertime:

And the linen is easy

☆

The Betty Trask Award gives £26,000 to the best writer of romantic fiction but lately critics had claimed the winners had been far too unromantic. Never mind, the new chairman of the judges Joanna Trollope vowed she would change things. The *Sunday Telegraph* said:

A Trollope rescues romance

☆

For a while there, it seemed Soho's Frith Street was THE place to eat. The food writers were queuing up to review its many excellent establishments. The *Sunday Telegraph* said it offered:

Mean cuisine
with street edibility

☆

But sometimes the task of the food writers isn't quite as easy as it seems. We all reckon we could swan into the latest eatery and offer our expert views but try being the *Sunday Telegraph* man reviewing Hong Kong's restaurants. There was deer's penis, dried oviduct of frog, caterpillar fungus and double-boiled turtle glue. The headline on his article was mild:

Waiter!
There's a horse in my soup

☆

After spending a break in the Cotswolds, home of weekending royals and bucolic sports, the *Sunday Telegraph*'s writer said he had been:

Amid hind parts
and coronets

☆

Holidaymakers travelling to exotic locations tend to poke their cameras and their camcorders into every nook and cranny to record the way that locals live. This can be disconcerting and the *Sunday Telegraph* suggested that they might be a little more discreet. It argued for some:

Shutter diplomacy

☆

The public footpaths of Britain have been disappearing in vast numbers over recent years as walkers desert them for more popular pursuits, like shopping. But footpaths still have some fierce devotees who are prepared to walk them and write about them to maintain interest in them. People like the *Sunday Telegraph*'s Byron Rogers whose piece was headlined:

One man and
his doggedness

☆

Sylvester Stallone is unusual among showbiz stars for giving revealing interviews. His piece in the *Sunday Telegraph*, in which he spoke about his family, was especially so. Recalling the sixties pop group the headline was:

Sly vs the family Stallone

☆

Stallone's affairs naturally make the headlines. He has a taste for big, Amazonian blondes. But when he announced his impending marriage to the latest, it was clear she had something extra. An aide told the *Sun* what this was and they used the memorable, if rather unkind, quote as their headline:

Angie has all Sly is looking
for in a wife … plus brains

☆

The biennial Venice festival was being organised by Achilles Bonito Oliva – 'Achilles the beautiful olive' in translation. His devotion to the more esoteric forms of art was dubbed 'socio–art-speak' by the *Sunday Telegraph* and its piece was headlined:

Achilles and
the jargonauts

☆

Neighbours were getting pretty fed up with their local opera singer who insisted upon practising her scales at home. The *Daily Mirror* headlined its story:

A real pain in the arias

☆

'Star Trek' devotees were shocked by the revelations in the *Daily Mirror* of the woman who played Lt Uhura. She claimed that its creator Gene Roddenberry had suggested a three-in-a-bed romp with her. The headline on the story was:

Three in a bed . . .
my final frontier with Mr Star Trek

☆

It's probably the lenient tax laws but a host of rock and roll stars have been setting up home in Ireland. It may not have the sun of Los Angeles but Dublin Bay, said the *Today* newspaper, was fast becoming Ireland's answer to Beverly Hills.

Shamrock 'n' roll

There were winners and losers when a diet campaign announced its awards. The booby prize, a statue with a ballooning stomach, was awarded to comedian Frank Carson who admitted that his diet of curries, fry-ups and beer hadn't left him looking exactly trim. The *Daily Star* headlined its story:

Gutcha awards

☆

Country music had a brief flirtation with the pop charts when both Sting and Jimmy Nail had top-selling hits. They were, said the *Guardian*, in the great tradition 'of people who have never smelt the sage brush or eaten their chuck under a prairie moon'. But they were the:

Fastest drawl
in the west

☆

The relationship between 'EastEnders' actress Gillian Taylforth and her boyfriend Geoff Knights made regular forays in the news. She finally left him after her chauffeur was beaten-up. It was, said the *Sun*, the:

Ender the road

☆

It never ceases to amaze us what showbiz stars will tell journalists — or at least what journalists claim they have been told. *Forrest Gump* star Tom Hanks apparently announced that the secret of his long-running marriage was that he and his wife Rita Wilson had a pact to 'always make time for hot, passionate sex'. The *Sun* called this:

Gumpy pumpy

Some stars make news even if they have done nothing. The latest picture of supermodel Elle Macpherson, for instance, claims acres of space regardless of there being any noteable event. At this point caption writers are put to work to scrape together some words to justify the picture.

A photograph of Macpherson playing tennis on the beach was used in the *Daily Mirror* – showing off her 'sets appeal' – under the headline:

Elle played

And *Today*:

Elle and high water

3

Sex

'Lord give me chastity, but not yet!'

St Augustine

For many months the word 'bonking' ruled supreme in headlines which necessarily require short words. The *Sun*, presumably fed up with the word, announced its demise with the headline:

Yuppies stop bonking and start porking

The word, however, failed to catch on and it wasn't long before 'bonking' returned with a vengeance. For instance, in the story about a 13-year-old boy caught having sex with a dinner lady on a dining-room table:

Boy, 13, bonks school
dinner lady on table

☆

When a middle-aged couple were caught having 'a sex romp' it was doubtful which gave the headline writers the bigger opportunity, the sex or the fact that it was in a Skoda. The *Daily Record* neatly captured both elements with:

A man Skoda do . . .

☆

A top QC, apparently nicknamed Rumpole by his colleagues, was accused in front of the Bar Council of being 'a sex pest'. The *Sun* told readers, headlining the story:

Rumpty of the Bailey

☆

The 52-year-old British grandmother who fell in love with a 27-year-old beach boy from The Gambia, received massive attention from the newspapers. Her problem getting the man an entry visa was headlined in the *Sun*:

Tribal and Strife

☆

With some stories alliteration seems to be the only sensible device when it comes to the headline. The barmaid who caused such a ruckus on Lundy Island was a case in point.
The *Daily Star* headline was:

The lusty lass of
Lundy laid our lads

☆

The *Daily Mirror* chose to focus upon her astrological interests:

Stargazing barmaid
Taurus apart

Sometimes the headline writer cannot resist putting the lot in the headline. Reminiscent of the old *News of the Word* headlines was this from the *Stockport Express Advertiser*:

King of Spain's manservant
was the naked sex slave
of a Peruvian top cop's
nightclub-owning former wife

The sex life of the fish 'is a cold, non-physical affair' the *Sunday Telegraph* told its readers. Worse, the sex life of the guppy is even more of a non-event. The headline was:

They call it guppy love

Mao Tse Tung's sex life was revealed in a documentary on BBC2. Women apparently felt honoured to be the object of his ardour. The *Leeds Weekly News*

announced the revelations with:

Mao He's Making Eyes At Me

☆

There were similar problems for a local dancing girl in Bournemouth who caught the eye of the ageing lothario Omar Sharif. Their inevitably brief fling was brought to the readers of the *Evening Echo* with the headline:

Omar he's making eyes at me

☆

Round-the-world solo sailor Mike Golding caused a stir when he revealed that he had a female companion on his lonely mission . . . a blow-up doll called Griselda.

The *Daily Star* headlined the story:

Hoist the Dolly Roger

☆

That classic summer headline 'Phew, What a Scorcher' got a re-working for *TV Weekly*'s review of the steamy opening episode of Joanna Trollope's Aga-saga 'The Rector's Wife'.

Pew, what a scorcher

☆

And in the week that the first bishop came out of the closet and announced his homosexuality and Rome softened its views on the subject, the *Guardian*'s weekend section 'Outlook' took a deep and penetrating look at the affair and headlined the piece:

Lipstick on their dog-collars

☆

Romantic liaisons in the aisles of the supermarket may seem unlikely but the *Glasgow Evening Times* claimed to have found a seething hotbed of trolley courting on St Valentine's Day and headlined the story:

Love lettuce straight from the 'mart

☆

Isabella Harrower won a divorce from her husband because of his filthy language. There were precious few words – mostly asterisks – in the *Daily Star*'s headline over the story:

F***! The F***** Wife Has F***** Off

☆

The world's first dating agency specially for 40-plus women was doing a roaring trade, the *Sun* told its readers under the headline:

ToyBoys 'Я' Us

☆

The world's first 'bonk bench' – a piece of sexual equipment designed to make variety the spice of life, got star billing in, where else, the *Daily Sport*, under this explicit headline:

Gym'll fux it!

The wet weather was having a serious effect on the breeding cycle of owls, the Press Association reported. The *Sheffield Star*, quick as a flash, responded with:

Too wet to woo

A court report about a jilted mum who took revenge on her cheating lover by throwing paint over his van was headlined in the *Wiltshire Gazette and Herald*:

Mum's revenge in an outburst of emulsion

When a top Wimbledon umpire ran off with a line-judge, the headline in the *Sun* was:

New Balls Please

☆

When the arc lights are switched on and the heady whiff of greasepaint is in the air, it appears leading ladies tend to fall for their cameraman. We think it's more to do with innate cunning. Flirting with the cameraman means he's more likely to show you in a flattering light. However, the story in the *Sunday Times* summed up the phenomenon:

Lights, camera, action . . .

Those few dots following the word action help to convey things that even a headline writer chooses not to say.

Britain's most romantic village – of course it probably isn't but when you come across a village called Lover the phrase is inescapable – has lost its Post Office; which means that the chance to frank romantic cards and letters from all over the country on Valentine's Day has also been lost.

The story was reported in the *Southern Daily Echo* thus:

Lover's Labour Lost

When the first Anglican women priests were ordained it was a simple headline for the *Bristol Evening Post*:

Equal rites

War broke out between bra manufacturers over who could make the bra with the, well, greatest uplift. Hundreds of pages swelled with the proud boasts and even prouder illustrations of the rival companies. The *Yorkshire Post* maintained a lofty approach to the story when it decided that it was time to write about the bra wars:

Twin piques as firms try to lift profit figures

☆

Those brassiere wars raged throughout most of 1994 with the manufacturers like Wonderbra leading the way. The *Daily Mirror* reported that waif-like model Kate Moss had taken to wearing one – unkindly pointing out that this seemed hardly necessary and even more unkindly headlining the story:

The bra hasn't done wonders for you, Kate!

☆

At the other end of the anatomy, the *Daily Mirror*'s fashion writers put together a piece on alluring fashions for shapely bottoms and called it:

Rear admirables

☆

Those lusty Chippendales caused a sensation wherever they went – at least, if you believed the headlines, they did. In the *York Journal* the approach to their testosterone tour was rather more aloof:

Good biceps, Mister Chipps

☆

Still in Yorkshire, where a man is a man even if he insists upon a slightly unusual garb. The *Wharfedale Observer* told readers about a man who had survived two World Wars and three beer shortages. He viewed them as roughly equal in hardship but when the photographer turned up, insisted upon dressing in a floral frock and straw hat. They announced:

Frock, horror, probe, it's a man in a dress

☆

Doncaster's main singles club was hit by an inexplicable outbreak of romance. More than half the members of the club, for unattached over-35s, had paired off, and four successive weddings had tilted the balance so much that they were considering accepting couples.

The *Guardian*, capitalizing upon the popular success of Hugh Grant's starring vehicle, headlined the story:

Four weddings could mean club's funeral

The film *Disclosure*, based on the Michael Crighton book which revolved around the sexual harassment of a MAN, had the feature writers out in force trying to discover whether this was a modern phenomenon or merely a good story-line for a book.

Lowri Turner, the *Sunday Mirror* columnist told readers that she hadn't yet noticed many men 'loitering around the photocopier choking back tears and biting their lips for fear of blurting out the dreadful truth of a female hand slipped surreptitiously up their trouser leg . . .' Her piece was headlined:

The gropes of wrath

☆

But a secretary who claimed that she had been sexually molested by her boss went to court in San Francisco and was apparently awarded a staggering £5 million. The *Daily Mirror* called it:

The £5 million fondle

☆

The latest trend on the ski slopes, reported the *Sun*, was naked skiing and to prove it they showed a photograph of a naked female skier, captioning it: 'Sight for thaw eyes.' The headline read:

Race you
to the bottom

☆

The *Guardian* profiled a woman it called a 'cyberfeminist'. Sadie Plant believed, they said, that the Internet would dismantle the unequal gender relations. Its headline?

Deadlier than the e-mail

☆

Why do women have affairs with priests? You may never have asked yourself the question but the *Guardian* did and talked to a number of people about the curious fascination which the clergy have for some women. It headlined the piece:

Caress me Father, for I have sinned

☆

So-called 'cheating' MPs were commonplace for a while and readers of some tabloids were regularly regaled with stories of their exploits. The mistress of one told the *News of the World* that he seduced her with soothing words and a cup of coffee! The *News of the World* headlined her revelations thus:

Bob seduced me with coffee then perked me up in bed

☆

And while on the subject, the mistress of MP David Mellor, Antonia de Sancha, found herself an acting role in a film about the 17th-century British composer Purcell. She played his wife. For *Today*, the news that she was cleaning up her reputation deserved headlines. This one, in fact:

The proof:
Purcell washes whiter

☆

The extraordinary story of the Bank of England deputy governor Rupert Pennant-Rea and his seemingly unbridled affair with a financial journalist, occupied the front pages for a few days and the inevitable headline arrived first in the *Sunday Mirror*.

The bonk of England

☆

The *News of the World* couldn't resist it either, using exactly the same headline. *Today* went for something a little different three days later when the man finally resigned.

Bank boss: bottom falls out
of his futures market

☆

Even the *Independent* got in on the act:

Reliable Rupert leaves
Old Lady in disgrace

☆

The affairs of a national orchestra got front-page billing

for a short while when it seemed that they got up to all sorts of sexual mischief while on tour. The *Sunday Mirror* told us the story with this headline:

Sexual overtures

☆

A barman was sacked by his wife, who ran the pub, after she discovered that he had been providing a service to three other women. The *Daily Star* told us:

Landlady sacks hubby who pulled girls instead of pints

☆

Sometimes headline writers just lose the plot. The *Daily Express* ran a story about a woman who was allegedly sacked after refusing to have sex with her boss. He was said to resemble, note that word, Reg Holdsworth who is a fictional character in 'Coronation Street'. Never mind that he wasn't Holdsworth nor that Holdsworth doesn't exist, the headline was:

Sacked for saying no to sex with Reg Holdsworth

☆

We can't do better with this one than to let you read the first paragraph of the story – a classic of its type. 'A bonking bandmaster faces the boot from the Army for making sweet music with six lovers behind his wife's back.' The story, which appeared in the *Sun*, quoted the bandmaster's wife thus: 'His job is to wave his stick in the Army band but he's wagged it once too often.'

The headline:

Horny Sgt out on his brass

☆

The key to success in TV, announced the *Guardian* writer Judy Rumbold after careful study of the latest American soap, was 'oiled bodies, toffee tans and very few clothes'. We all know what she was talking about:

The bottom line on Baywatch

☆

A major lottery winner had been cheating on his wife, the *Sun* announced. His name helped them call him:

National Rotter Lee

☆

It all sounded rather like a story from Maupassant. A reformed prostitute wrote to President Mitterand asking him to save the career of the lawyer who was forced to retire after setting up home with her. The *Sunday Telegraph* told the story under this headline:

Judge pays price after giving his heart to a tart

☆

The owner of a fleet of swanky stretch limos was interviewed by the *Daily Mirror* about the sort of people who used his service and what they got up to. Apparently it wasn't uncommon for them to use his cars to have sex and he had to ban stiletto heels. Why? The headline explained it:

No stilettos in my stretch limo please . . . they wreck the roof

A mother-of-two who bought a double bed for romantic sessions with her lover launched a High Court battle to get it back when they split up. The *Sun* announced:

For bedder or worse!

4

News

4

News

'Newspaper editors are men who separate the wheat from the chaff and then print the chaff'

Adlai Stevenson

Sometimes it doesn't do to question too deeply the words in a headline. They're there to convey meaning, if not precision. When the *Sun* got hold of a story about frogs being slaughtered by cars on a dangerous crossing, it headlined the story:

Halt!
Major toad ahead

Frogs, of course, are not toads but you got the message.

☆

Visitors to Canterbury Cathedral were told that they would have to pay an entrance fee for the first time. The notion

---
68

of paying to enter the House of God went down badly with many, and the *Daily Mail* headlined its story:

Dearer my God
to thee at
£2 a head

☆

Switzerland's soldiers, it seems, are ready and alert for the merest hint of the outbreak of war. Mind you, some of them will have to get to the front line, wherever it is, on their bikes, according to the *Daily Star* which headlined its story:

Cycle-ogical warfare

☆

A woman who had been close to the Libyan leader claimed he might be homosexual. Might be, you note, but nevertheless such was the feeling about him at the time that this was enough for the *Sun* to headline its story:

'Mad dog' Gaddafi's
a raving poofter

☆

The arrival of a cuckoo in the calendar – the thirteenth zodiacal sign – wasn't so bad. But its name gave headline writers a stiff challenge. *The Times* rose splendidly to the task with a little help from the sixties rock opera *Hair*.

Is this the dawning of the age of Ophiuchus?

☆

A Viking longships regatta on Wearside gave the *Sunderland Echo* fun with:

Norse day out in fjord fiesta

☆

Birds of prey are being encouraged to mate along a nature trail at Anglesey, the *Liverpool Daily Post* told readers, under this:

Owls should go to it to woo!

☆

The closure of so many town-centre, specialist shops in the wake of out-of-town superstores has been a recurring theme for many local newspapers over the last few years. Bargain hunters swarmed to the closing-down sale of an electrical shop in Epsom after the *Epsom and Banstead News* left readers in little doubt about how it felt:

Cry now while shops last

☆

Take time out from your busy life for anti-stress meditation classes, the *Hartlepool Mail* told readers:

Buddha can you spare the time

Thieves cleaned out a farmer's stock of sheep taking more than sixty from his field in Knutsford. The local *Guardian* newspaper told readers:

Flock, stock and barrel

The claims of a new second-hand car dealer chain to give buyers a fair deal brought this slightly ironic headline out of the *Sun*:

Honest engine

The question mark at the end of the headline spoiled it slightly but the *South London Press* was anxious about the jobs of Texas DIY store workers after the £290 million takeover. It asked:

Texas Chainstore Massacre?

Nick Leeson's role in the Barings collapse was still unclear in the early days of the story but while he was on the run newspapers felt able to take him to task. The *Daily Star* called him:

Long Gone Silver

one day and then told him:

Come back You Little Banker

the next.

☆

While the *Sun*, believing he might be on a 'paradise island' off the coast of Thailand – surely not just because of its headline possibilities – asked:

Where the Phuket is he?

☆

A police chief is to teach reformed Arab terrorists how to keep the peace, the *Sun* told us, under:

Yasser, that's my bobby!

☆

Advertisers have long been keen to claim that your pets can distinguish their pet food from any other. But a survey published in the *Sun* was less helpful.

They all taste like dogs' breakfasts!

☆

The arrival of a cheese factory in Leeds would boost the job prospects of locals, so naturally the *Yorkshire Post* welcomed the news with:

What a friend we have in cheeses

Gardening advice from the *Evening Standard* on how to produce the best lawn:

When the turf gets going . . .

Fishermen in the north-east feared that Spanish fishermen would quit their own overfished waters and flood the Irish Sea if the EU rules were changed. The *Whitehaven News* summed the story up brilliantly with:

Local fishermen fear all Basques in one exit

Three racehorses, a Shetland pony and a llama staged their own version of the Grand National over the roads of Over Wire near Blackpool. With echoes of a fifties pop song the *Evening Gazette*, in inspired form, told readers about the:

Llama drama ding dong!

Eleven cats and now two new-born kittens had been locked in a house for up to two years without sanitation. It had undoubtedly been, as the *New Forest Post* told readers:

Black hole of cat-clutter

☆

Sometimes just telling the story is bizarre enough, as readers of the *North-West Evening Mail* discovered when it splashed a story about MoD shells bombarding prawn fishermen's nets.

Army Shelled Our Prawns

☆

And when the driver of a Datsun car lost control and it flew into a house, the *Solihull Times* told readers:

It's raining Datsun cogs

☆

It was the bizarre task of the *Observer* to tell its readers about a mongrel dog which survived only by eating part of the leg of its dead owner. In one of the more extraordinary headlines of 1995 it announced:

Corpse saves dog

☆

A kind and concerned local lady rescued two geese from a

pond after they had been savaged by dogs. Once they were
back in good health she needed to find owners and the *Hull
Daily Mail* was happy to help.

All we are saying is
give geese a chance

☆

The extraordinary collapse of Franklands, where part
of the Sussex village suddenly started disappearing
into the sea, might have been averted if a dam had
been built to hold back the sea. The *Today* newspaper,
with echoes of *Gone With The Wind*, told the story under
the headline:

Franklands my fear,
we should have had a dam

☆

Grass on the roofs of eco-houses in Thamesmead saves
hundreds of pounds by providing added insulation. The
local *Mercury* newspaper warned:

People in grass houses
shouldn't mow lawns

☆

The arrival of the new Sonata motor car from Korea
gave headline writers a treat, especially since few
motoring writers raved about it. *Health View* was

typical of the headlines:

Let's Be Frank,
Sonata

☆

The *Sunday Times* looked at the future of Jaguar cars and concluded that the release of its new saloon car signalled make or break time for the marque. No doubt about its conclusions from the headline which announced:

Last chance saloon

☆

Soaring smoked salmon sales in south London were reported in the *South London Press* with the headline:

Salmon Rush Day

☆

Poor little Lisa Potter would have to wait two and a half years for corrective dental treatment, the *Lancashire Evening Telegraph* announced with this flourish:

The Moana of Lisa
as Smile is Hidden

☆

The refusal by insurers to offer cover for the bottom of Mr Methane – whose flatulent performances of 'Twinkle,

Twinkle, L~~~~ Star' entertained locals in Macclesfield –
gave the normally austere *Independent* a chance to smile:

Mr Methane's tunes
put the wind up insurers

☆

The risk of rollover in jeeps has been a controversial subject
but the *Bridgewater Mercury* still managed a rock and roll
tone to its headline:

Rollover rate proven

☆

The extraordinary story of the theft of 150 sets of the sexual
organs of stags seemed ready made for the headline writers.
The *Scotsman* rose to the challenge with this gently
suggestive headline:

Wily raid at game dealer's

☆

Middlesbrough Council's decision to cut back on toilet rolls
in public lavatories – just one roll between five cubicles –
was brilliantly summed up by the *Sunday Sun* in Newcastle
with this headline:

A-tissue, a-tissue,
we're four rolls down

☆

Christmas brings a flood of smashing headlines with the writers vying with one another to provide the top seasonal cracker.

When a dog in a Santa Claus hat joined carol singers in Benfleet, Essex, an inspired sub-editor on the *Evening Echo* responded with:

Bark! The herald angels sing . . .

In Bournemouth, charity fund-raising to provide beds and bedding for the homeless at Christmas was a major talking point – and no less in the splendid local evening newspaper, the *Evening Echo*. When a Band Aid-style concert was announced to raise money for the cause, the headline came right out of the top drawer:

Duvet know it's Christmas?

Meanwhile, in Hull, schizophrenia was the topic. The *West Hull Shopper* warned readers that at Christmas we all tend to show evidence of split personalities – the romantic, full of Christmas spirit side, and the ratty, resentful side; which gave the sub-editor just the material he needed for a play on the famous line from *A Christmas Carol*:

Christmas – God bless us every two!

Even the sports writers were in on the act. In Bath, the likely retirement of boxer Kirkland Laing – who kindly spelled his name in just the right fashion – was written up in the *Bath Evening Chronicle* under the headline:

Auld Laing syne

☆

Meanwhile, in Southampton councillors decided to spend £7,000 on special illuminations to convert the city centre trees into Christmas trees. The *Southern Daily Echo* summed it all up:

Deck the boughs
with lots of lolly

☆

And still with the Christmas theme, British Airways entered the seasonal spirit by putting a red Rudolph nose on the cockpit of the special Christmas flight of a Boeing 737 from Manchester Airport. The story in the *Manchester Evening News* was headlined:

Rudolph's the
red-nosed plane, dear

☆

Low attendance at a trade exhibition was exercising the minds of the journalists on *IBM Today*. These, you must admit, were minds with an esoteric bent. Mussorgsky, for some reason, came to mind for the heading:

Empty pitches
at an exhibition

☆

The anniversary of Arnhem stuck firmly in the minds of headline writers for a while. Over a piece about talking books, and the authors' protests about the degree to which they were being cut down to fit conveniently onto cassettes, the *Sunday Telegraph* used the headline:

Talking books are
abridged too far,
angry authors claim

☆

Meanwhile in Hartlepool a schoolboy was ordered to learn the part of King Lear for a school play. This being one of the most arduous, and lengthy parts in Shakespeare, the lad took one look at his chunk of the script and tore out all but two pages – learning just eight lines in the process.

The *Hartlepool Mail* told the story under the headline:

Abridged too far

☆

DIY builders normally imperil only themselves but in Oxford a family was engaged upon building work which threatened the stability of neighbours' homes.

The neighbours naturally complained. It was just unfortunate for the family that they had an unusual name – and that the *Oxford Mail* picked up on the story:

Neighbours are shaken by the Balls

The heir to a fortune had been sought far and wide and he was finally tracked down to a trailer park to which he had escaped and where he was living in a jeep. He just preferred it that way. The *Torquay Express* expressed some surprise in its story which it headlined:

Heir on a Jeep fling

We've all wondered what subject we might be capable of tackling on 'Mastermind'. One man settled upon his favourite very swiftly – beer. When he made it to the competition the *Sun* headlined a story about him:

I've started so ale finissshh

The lifeboat was called out off the south coast to rescue a Swedish family after the kitchen in their yacht fell out of the bottom of the boat. Honest!

The *Southern Daily Echo* told the story under this headline:

Kitchen sink drama

☆

Sleaze in the public utilities was a big issue for everyone in the news business. Moans about soaring costs and the hardship created by them were contrasted with the big salaries and bonuses being earned by the people at the top. Nowhere did a newspaper sum up the problem better than the *Southampton Advertiser* with:

The plight of the charge brigade

☆

And there were some pretty desperate stories being told about the problems of those people who had bought homes and later found themselves to be in the path of the Channel Tunnel rail route. Unable to sell and horrified about the consequences of staying, they were pressing for compensation – but many didn't get it.

The *Daily Telegraph* told the tragic story with this poignant headline:

Families find only blight at the end of the tunnel

☆

A new Korean 4x4 jeep was extensively reviewed and several newspapers managed to build its name into the headline. But none better than the *Evening Gazette* in Middlesbrough with:

Je suis une Rocsta

And another new product was causing some excitement in Scotland where that favourite drink Irn Bru was being challenged by a rival called Rivets. Brewed by a gentleman called Dr Okhai from Tayside, the new drink was being heavily marketed and promoted. The *Scotsman* wrote at some length about the battle for supremacy in this key soft-drink market under the clever headline:

Okhai the brew,
or just a rusty rival?

If Prince Charles has a pig farm on his extensive estates then he might like to take advice from the *Yorkshire Post* which regaled readers with a story about new techniques for fattening pigs. You talk to them. Rather like flowers, really. It headlined its story:

Chat up a pig . . .
and see the last of
the slimmer swine

Dr Carey's frequent speeches on the state of our world

regularly hit the headlines. In one he came to some pretty depressing conclusions about the condition of youth today – barbershop stuff really but since he was a leading clergyman the *Observer* wrote it up under the headline:

Youth hasn't got a prayer – Carey

☆

And one of the problems, it seems, is an obsession with video games. If we are worried about them here, you should see what's been going on in America where a Senate debate on the topic was heated, to say the least. The newsagents weekly *CTW* reported the story under the headline:

Washington, our dirty linen in public

☆

Pest control officers were called out to help free a trapped cat – a problem which proved intractible . . . for a while. *Environmental Issues*, the magazine produced by Rentokil reported the story thus:

Once more with feline

☆

When a beach inspector managed to smash up the bike belonging to a perfectly innocent boy, the council, after some while, finally apologised. We don't know whether they offered any recompense but we suspect they did after the newspapers got onto the story.

The *Bournemouth Advertiser* told readers:

Inspector Remorse

☆

The retirement of long-serving employee Roma Potter from British Gas was recorded faithfully in *Unison Week*, the company newspaper under the headline:

Arrivederci Roma

☆

Alex the alligator found himself a little weary after his perambulations across a North Carolina swamp and he took a ninety minute nap – in the middle of the main road around it. This naturally held up traffic in both directions and gave headline writers some fun.

The *Daily Star* told the story under the headline:

Please get that
old croc off the road

☆

Some curious characters came out of the woodwork with *perestroika* in Russia. Vladimir Zhirinovsky, the right-wing politician, announced that it was his ambition to see Russian troops washing their boots in the Indian Ocean – a feat which would have hardly endeared him to countries like Iran and Pakistan, never mind the rest of us.

The *Independent on Sunday* told its readers about this dangerous new force in Russian politics under the headline:

These boots aren't made for watering

Choristers were in short supply in Salisbury when the cathedral choir was looking for youngsters to help them in the production of works composed by Jonathan Dove. *Sarum Link*, the official newspaper of the diocese, told its readers, perhaps inevitably:

O for the song of a Dove!

Share ownership plans – like many other forms of investment – have their risks. It's the duty of personal finance writers to tell readers about this, but that doesn't mean they have to be stoney-faced about it.

The *Daily Telegraph*'s 'Money Go Round' pages wrote about employee share ownership schemes called Esops warning:

When Esops are no happy fable but a grim tale

Travelling showmen were concerned about their treatment by the taxman who was demanding that they pay full motor taxation on their equipment because they transported it by road.

Motor Transport reported the story thus:

Too many swings and no roundabouts say fair men

☆

When a mock Civil War battle was disrupted by fire in the car park, caused after a canon barrel ignited dry stubble, the *Daily Mail* captured the spirit with:

Cavalier up in flames: Roundheads suspected

☆

Drama in the local Indian restaurant when a man's curry went up in smoke. The *Milton Keynes Citizen* resorted to a song title for its headline:

Tears on his pilau

☆

Still on restaurants, those lucky people the restaurant critics have a high old time swilling around the top nosheries on expenses and they even have the luxury of skilled headline writers to add bite to their reviews. The *Sunday Times* review of a Japanese restaurant is a case in point:

Nippon tuck

☆

The *Evening Standard*'s excellent restaurant critic was equally well-served by her sub-editors when she reviewed the endless little delicacies served up in a Sri Lankan restaurant.

The pittu patter
of tiny feats

And when a potato lorry crashed injuring its driver the *Kidderminster Times* couldn't resist recalling that staple of the kitchen larder:

Potato lorry driver
hurt in smash

The delights of Dartmouth were described in a travel article in the *Gravesend Reporter* thus:

Devon Sent

☆

And when proposals were made for drivers to have their photographs attached to driving licences, the

Greenock Telegraph did a poll of readers to find their reactions to the idea. Their approval was evident from the headline:

ID aye!

☆

A jobless man's unfortunate motoring experiences left him without the backing of his insurance company, a plight which the *Evening Gazette*, Blackpool, summed up with:

Third party, ire and left!

☆

Spare a thought for ambulance crews. TV's 'Casualty' shows just how difficult and sometimes dangerous the job is but they haven't come up with a plot half as bizarre as this one.

A crew was sent to an accident but was routed by a pair of geese. The police were called in to help and found that by this time the geese had been reinforced by a mad goat. All was revealed in a story in the *Caterham Mirror* with the headline:

Paramedics sent pecking and geese get the Bill too

☆

When the Nationwide Building Society sold its 300 estate agencies for a mere £1, a mathematically minded sub-editor on the *Independent* did his sums and announced:

Estate agents
are three a penny

Beer distributor George Swanson left precise instructions. When he died he was buried placed in the driving seat of his beloved 1984 Chevrolet Corvette. There were two driving caps on the back seat and red roses on the roof. The *Fortean Times* headlined its account of the bizarre burial thus:

Rust in Peace

Bad taste? Not about somebody who asked for Englebert Humperdink's 'Please Release Me' to be played at the funeral, it isn't.

Virgin boss Richard Branson won over £600,000 libel damages from rivals British Airways who were told to apologise for its 'dirty tricks' campaign against the airline. The *Sun* headlined the story:

Virgin screws BA

Advice to smokers from the *Bournemouth Evening Echo* suggested that there is something maternal about the desires of smokers:

Smokers are born suckers

Animal services in churches have become quite fashionable. One of the first was in Dorset where the *Evening Echo* announced:

Animals went in pew by pew

Anyone know what a subwoofer is? A new speaker system from a company called Mission which apparently boasts one – or possibly even two – was given the once over by the experts on *What Satellite TV*. This, it decided, was a case of:

Missionary positioning

We've become big pasta eaters in recent years – not yet ready to challenge the vast consumption of the Italians but enough to attract a piece in *Checkout*, the grocery magazine, which headlined its story:

Pasta la vista

And the same idea came to the sub-editor on the *Bristol Journal*. Lord Astor's visit to Bristol was soon followed by his departure from Bristol, with few people any the wiser or better off. The *Journal* announced obliquely:

Astor-la Vista!

Cider sales are booming again, news which gives great heart to the West Country where cider has always been taken seriously. The *Independent*'s City pages told the story of the resurgence with this neat headline:

In cider dealing

There was strong criticism in the *Press and Journal*, Aberdeen, for the lack of an investigative edge on Gaelic Television. Its story was headlined:

Journalist bites
the bulletins

The Children In Need Appeal raised money for a host of important causes. The *Banstead Herald* looked at its local child-care facilities with a picture which showed two tiny tots crawling through pipes at their local centre:

Children on
knees appeal

The complicated matters dealt with by the more technical magazines provide a real test for sub-editors trying to sum up the story. *What Satellite TV* looked at the need for better service for those subjected to poor TV signals on variable band widths in some areas. What on earth to say in the headline? This is what they came up with:

Something for the weak end

The threats by German bureaucrats to ban British beef didn't go down well with some Brits and the promise of retaliation if such a ban was imposed was reported in the *Sunderland Echo* with the headline:

Beef burghers may land in frying pan!

City speculators were swift to mark down shares in Tottenham Hotspur Football Club after it revealed that pre-tax profits in its first six months had slumped. *The Times* announced:

Spurs down at half-time

Star graduate Lucy Samways announced in her local newspaper that she intended to take up flying; which was enough for the *Epsom and Ewell Herald* sub-editor to announce:

Lucy in sky's a diamond

A 14-year-old lurcher hound deserves a rather gentler form of exercise than stiff walks. And that is what Sam has decided upon. He no longer goes out for a stroll with owner Sandra Mason, he prefers the Tyneside Metro. Readers of the *Northern Echo* were told the story under the headline:

Hound of the faster thrills.

It was a bitter-sweet day in Wallsend as the last vessel to be built in the dockyards sailed gracefully out of the Swan Hunter yard. It was captured by *The Times* under the headline:

Last act of the dying Swan

Pupils at Abbotsford School in Kenilworth trooped in two-by-two for their special Noah's Ark week captured delightfully in the *Leamington Courier* with the headline:

Ark that heralds playful things

The threat to bulldoze villagers' allotments to make way

for a clinic was highlighted in the *Wilmslow Express Advertiser* under the imaginative headline:

The cabbage patch snatch

☆

Coal bosses who had just closed the County Durham Colliery were applying for permission to store coal on the site and villagers at Easington, worst hit by the closure, suspected that this would be foreign coal. It would be rubbing their noses in it, they felt.

Not much doubt how the *Sunderland Echo* felt about it all either. It headlined the story:

Pile of spite

☆

A rare and exotic hoopoe, which should have been wintering in Africa, took up residence in a back garden in Gosport, Hampshire, after straying off course. Birdwatchers flocked from all over to see its pink-striped plumage, curved beak and fanlike crest.

But a cat got there first, said the *Daily Mail*, which summed it all up:

Birdwatchers are crestfallen as a peckish cat kills the curiosity

☆

A brewery dray horse which had developed a taste for beer was given a Christmas present of forty-eight cans by the brewery bosses. All of which gave the *Bournemouth Evening Echo* the headline:

He's a draught horse

The survey on sex by the Office of Population, Census and Surveys, commissioned by Mrs Thatcher, was a dry old publication full of statistics, charts and demographics. The *Guardian* wanted to know why we couldn't be more like the French and treat sex as a subject for enjoyment and fun.

Copulation, Censors and Surveys

And in France a plan to change the funding of schools brought a million people out to protest in Paris. But all the sleaze of recent years in Britain had failed to bring even a breath of public protest, said a letter writer in the *Guardian*. And he suggested that if John Major really wanted to get us back to basics then encouraging political awareness should be part of our national curriculum. The headline?

Down in London
and out in Paris

A nimble-fingered priest using applique and braids created a new set of vestments for himself at his church in Hatfield,

Hertfordshire. The *Bournemouth Evening Echo* told us:

Whatever ye sew so shall ye reap

'God moves in Strangeways his wonders to perform' the *Lincolnshire Echo* told readers. Former convicts who had been involved in the Strangeways riots had turned to God following those grim and traumatic days and were now aiming to win over converts. Its headline was:

Convert convicts tell all

The world's top organisation for clowns was searching for a new home for its valuable artefacts and memorabilia after being kicked out of their old base in east London. The *Yorkshire Post* told the story under the headline:

Homeless clowns loiter within tent

A policewoman writing in the magazine *Police Review* defied all politically correct rules by telling her colleagues that naughty nicknames for WPCs were all right so long as they could call PCs by similarly naughty names. It's not an idea which will find favour with most we suspect, especially after the *Daily Mirror* headlined the story:

WPC thunder thighs

Besieged by rising crime, states across the whole of America are looking to bring back corporal punishment in the hope that a good flogging might do what a quiet talking to and a holiday in Africa clearly doesn't. The *Daily Star* told the story under the headline:

Whack to the future

☆

And some evidence to suggest that the same policy might be welcomed in the UK came with the story about the policeman who faced the sack after thumping a yob who said that he'd like to throw the PC's baby daughter out of a train window.

Thousands of telephone calls of support for the PC came into newspapers in the following days. The *Daily Mirror* suggested that sacking the policeman would be:

Cuff justice

☆

A woman who sent the boyfriend who cheated on her a dead rat was unrepentant when the newspapers caught up with her. 'I wanted to buy him something that told him exactly how I felt,' she explained.

The *Sun* had a headline which did the job too:

Rodents are dead,
Violets are blue,
I sent you this rat,
Cos you were untrue

☆

An innocent couple, arrested at gunpoint, were awarded £37,000 compensation and this headline from *Today*:

Blunder Arrest

New York policewoman Carol Shaya was an arresting sight in *Playboy* magazine. Well, for most she was. Her bosses were more particular and sacked her for bringing the force embarrassment and disgrace. The *Sun* called it:

Hill Street Phews

The Advertising Standards Authority was asked to rule on whether or not the *Independent* could continue to run its campaign boasting of editorial independence now that it was owned by various large media groups. The ASA decided it couldn't. Heaven help the *Independent* if someone reports it under the Trades Descriptions Act, then. It might have to change its name and not just its advertising campaign.

The *Guardian*, a rival, headlined the story:

The Independent
It isn't . . .

The Barings débâcle was one of those stories that ran and ran. The *Aberdeen Press and Journal* told readers about the Dutch banking group ING buying the collapsed bank. Its headline:

Barings
goING goING gone

☆

A farmer appeared in court charged with deliberately driving his tractor into a police car on the A452. The jury found him not guilty on the charge. The *Daily Telegraph* announced:

Farmer cleared of ramming

Ewe have to think about it!

☆

Soap giant Unilever announced plans to go into Vietnam – a country which it reckoned had enormous potential. The *Liverpool Echo* left readers in no doubt why it thought there was such a big opportunity:

Soap giant takes on
the Viet Pong

☆

A beer row in which a brewery was accused of serving Courage Directors bitter under the name Wych-wood Barbarian got the Campaign for Real Ale hot under the collar. They felt that real ale drinkers were being fooled. *What's Brewing*, their newspaper, felt even more strongly about it. It asked:

Con on the Barbarian?

☆

The Pope's visit to Manila to say mass attracted a four-million strong crowd. *Today* newspaper was impressed and headlined its story:

That's what you call a Mass

☆

But after they had all left, the *Today* photographer stayed behind and his pictures of the rubbish which remained made the next day's paper. A young boy was photographed scavenging through a forest of mess under the headline:

Now that's what you call a mess

☆

An Indian woman who had her whole wardrobe stolen by burglars begged for its return. Especially important to her was her wedding sari.

The *Milton Keynes Citizen* reported the story under the slightly unsympathetic headline:

Whose sari now?

☆

'From Glasgow to Bosnia they drove, the most shambolic do-gooders this side of Mr Bean' said *Scotland on Sunday*, introducing its article about a pop group who risked life and limb to perform in Tuzla during the height of the conflict there. The headline?

24 hours in Tuzla

☆

Sunday Telegraph columnist Oliver Pritchett wrote his column one week about the art of apologising. His article was, itself, an apology laced with deep humility for his own sins. The headline writer faced with this extended *mea culpa* offered:

Sorry
with a cringe on top

☆

The severe flooding in northern Europe last winter claimed acres of coverage in the newspapers. It was serious, frightening and potentially economically ruinous. But after days of shock, horror headlines there was a need for something slightly lighter and *Today*, in an article about the flooding in Germany, came up with the headline:

The eau de Cologne

☆

A four man syndicate celebrated its success in the national lottery – sharing £16.2 million with 132 others. There was just a trace of envy in their celebrations – they had at first thought they were the only winners. *Kent Today* covered the story, briefly, and headlined it:

It's all four won but not one for all!

There was a darker side to the national lottery. A heartbroken father killed himself after discovering that his winning £1 million lottery ticket had expired. The *Independent* wondered what had happened to a nation where the failure to win a million pounds can do such a thing. Its lengthy headline asked poignantly:

Once, we sought salvation in religion. Now, 10 million prayers are raised for a National Lottery jackpot win – and when that hope is dashed, a man like Tim O'Brien takes his life . . . Have we all gone lottery mad?

The *Daily Mirror* carried the same story but said bluntly:

£1m loser

The Eiffel Tower was getting a new lick of paint. The *Wolverhampton Express and Star* wrote a piece about just what was involved in giving France's biggest Gallic symbol a facelift. It headlined the story:

Mon Dieu-lux

☆

Computer buffs were given a run-down on Windows and OS/2 operating systems in Slough's *Observer Midweek* computing column. It said:

The wizard of OS

☆

Guided tours offer some bizarre experiences but a tour around York's ancient and modern lavatories takes the biscuit. The *Liverpool Daily Post* was equally amazed and told its readers about this curiously Gallic fascination with public lavatories under the headline:

Now it's to loos le trek

☆

The humble tin can has been overtaken by a host of new ways of preserving food. For a while there it almost looked as though it was going to die-out. But *Independent Retail News*, the magazine of the grocery world, reported on a revival in its fortunes under the headline:

Tin can rally

Lord Lucan – dead or disappeared. The story had been written a hundred times and each theory has its believers. *Today* newspaper ran a series of articles investigating the disappearance of the fugitive earl. In one it claimed to have traced him to an African hideaway. The headline screamed:

Lucan, the wildebeest years

But there was more. A sneaky little sub-headline said:

Hot gnus, *Today* trails the fugitive Earl to his African hideaway, or is it just a Lucanlike?

The Russians are buying anything they can that is western. The value to them of our goods lies not only in their innate use but, more particularly, as a status symbol. One of the latest hotly sought-after commodities, reported *Scotland on Sunday*, was their own national soft drink, Irn Bru. It announced:

Back in the Irn BrUSSR,

The remains of a previously unknown species of two-legged dinosaur were found in south-east France. It was probably a good jumper, *The Times* told us, under the headline:

100m-year-old jumper found

☆

A postman appeared in court in Wales on a reckless driving charge. He told magistrates that he blacked out with the pain of his tight trousers rubbing against his manhood.

His explanation didn't do him much good but it helped the headline writers enormously:

The *Daily Star* headlined it:

Postman Splat

While the *Sun* called him:

Postman Pants

☆

The wife of Lonrho tycoon Tiny Rowland announced that she was to sue a writer whose book about her husband said some unkind things about her. But on consulting her lawyers she was told that it hadn't 'sufficiently abused her' and she withdrew. The *Guardian* said:

Mrs Rowland discovers
a wife's place is not in court

☆

Disputes between the islanders of Eigg and their eccentric

laird Keith Schellenberg were coming to a head, reported the *Mail on Sunday* under the perhaps predictable headline:

Eigg comes to the boil

Workers at the German owned Osram light-bulb factory near Oldham were told that if they wanted VE Day as a bank holiday like the rest of the country it would be deducted from their Christmas vacation. An outraged *Daily Express* headlined the story:

VE have ways of making you work

Police had to borrow a saw from neighbours to free a teenager stuck in the cat flap of his father's house.

The *Express and Star*, Wolverhampton, headlined the story:

Cat-flap teenager cried 'let miaowt'

The *Evening Standard* had the same story but headlined it:

Catflap man: 'Let miaow–t'

The *Daily Mirror* announced:

I'm feline silly

☆

And while on the subject of cats, Thomas the kitten had a narrow escape after getting stuck in the washing machine at his home near Sunderland.

The *Sunderland Echo* told its readers the story under the headline:

Cat in a hot-spin-goof

☆

An elderly lady who had booked herself in for a hairdo wasn't going to let anything get in the way – not even a suspended parking bay, the pavement or a brick wall. She drove her car through the lot in London's Berkeley Street. The story which appeared in the *Daily Mail* was headlined:

Miss an appointment for a hairdo? Not me, I just crash and go

When the centuries-old Durham Chorister School decided to break with tradition and accept girls, the *Sunderland Echo* announced:

School takes hers as well as hymns

☆

An insurance company announced plans to try and stop written-off cars finding their way back onto the roads after bodged repairs. *Motor Trader* told readers:

Bid to end toll from ringing

☆

A lady bus driver gave a cabbie a piece of her mind when he obstructed her bus. But instead of being upset by her ripe language he confessed that he was at fault and quite admired her for it. *Kent Today* summed it up with:

A street spar flamed desire for bus driver

☆

A number of people were hurt and huge traffic jams built up when cars skidded on the millions of dried peas which had spilled from a truck in Belgium. The *Mail on Sunday* called it:

Peas and queues

☆

Visitors kept tripping over the one-inch high plaque on the deck of HMS *Victory* which marked the spot at which Lord Nelson fell in the Battle of Trafalgar.

It was, said the *Mail on Sunday*, an:

Accident plaque spot

Financial whizz-kid Nick Leeson always showed promise for his future profession, the *Sun* told us, under a picture of him at 14 posing in the stocks at a medieval exhibition.

He wanted to be in stocks

☆

Good news from brewers Courage whose second-half figures perked up the City and gave *The Times'* head-line writer an opportunity which was seized with both hands.

Courage serves up
a better half

☆

Sometimes the coincidence is so great that a headline writer almost has no choice. Take the story in the *Scotsman* property pages which announced that the village of Wattston was going to get a new estate called Sherlock Park. Irresistible isn't it?

Sherlock homes
for Wattston

☆

Smart thinking from Eastern Gas's magazine *Cable* which told how the battle to increase gas sales was hotting up. It was headlined:

It's therm warfare

Insurance companies decided that if people wanted to smoke they would have to pay higher life assurance premiums to take some of the risk. The *Guardian* said:

Smokers told
to cough up

A surgeon who stayed at home while a junior doctor tried to find treatment for a dying man, came in for big and largely critical headlines. The *Daily Mirror* called him:

Doctor Dolittle

Jonathan Bean was as accident prone as his TV namesake. Wherever he went, anywhere in the world, disaster followed. The *Daily Mirror* said:

Bean there . . .
done it in!

The book written by kidnap victim John McCarthy and his girlfriend Jill Morrell went straight to the top of the bestsellers list and seemed to be making them a fortune. The *Guardian*'s article was headlined:

Hostage to fortune

The *Oldham Advertiser* announced that a local art gallery had benefited to the tune of £60,000 from the Arts Council's Sunrise Fund. Its headline:

Loadsamonet

☆

Dudley school cook Manohar Morgan was sacked after it was reported that children hated his curries so much they ate fish fingers in preference. Apparently the curries got progressively hotter and spicier until they were too fiery for the children. The *Birmingham Post* headlined its story:

Naan but the brave dared sample a Morgan curry

☆

A code of practice which would finally crack down on the cowboys of the bailiff business was long overdue, reported *Public Finance* magazine under the headline:

Sounding the debt knell

☆

Sheffield's massive £25 million Bourbon Street redevelopment collapsed leaving a host of red faces. The *Sheffield Telegraph* announced the news with this headline:

Bourbon on the rocks

Bringing art to the community in North Staffordshire meant a combined effort between the artistic community, local firms, councils and other organisations. The teamwork impressed the *North Staffs Advertiser* who said:

It's surreally good day out

☆

Masterpieces of a different sort were being hunted down by a specialist who haunted the salerooms to find works of art which the experts hadn't spotted. He regularly picked up valuable paintings for a song, said the *Sunday Telegraph* under this headline:

Trader of the lost art

☆

Alastair Simms has a rare skill. Not only is he one of only eleven brewery coopers in Britain, said the *Licensee and Morning Advertiser*, but, as their picture showed:

He really knows his adze from his elbow

☆

Spare a thought for the man who gave his beloved Toyota a kiss but forgot quite what a cold night it had been and found himself stuck to the bonnet. The *Sun* was there to record the embarrassing affair under the headline:

Lips stick on my corolla

A group of students were planning to set up their own brewery at Sunderland University and the *Sunderland Echo* called it:

Brew-niversity of Sunderland

A housing association came up with a bright new way to ease the housing shortage. It offered council tenants the chance to retire to Spain. For rent of £60 per week they would get fully furnished two-bedroom apartments on the Costa Blanca. The *Daily Mirror* called them:

Señor Citizens

Meanwhile for those staying at home, instead of the Spanish sun and sand, what about some coal dust between your toes? Tempting tours of coal pits and colliery cottages were being offered for those bored with foreign parts. Said the *Daily Star*, how about the:

Costa del coal

The Times property writer looked at the conversion of a listed watermill in Norfolk into a home. It was, said the headline with no apologies to George Eliot, a case of:

Gloss on the mill

BBC radio presenter John Humphreys has a reputation for rough stuff with the politicians but, it seems, he's just the same with crooks. He woke to find his home being burgled and, completely naked, chased the intruder out. The *News of the World* said:

Nudesman John
sees off burglar

Once they were simple, harmless things full of entertaining characters called Goofy and Lord Snooty but an influx of violent and sexually explicit comics from Japan was flooding the country, warned the *Sunday Telegraph* under the headline:

Japan's cruelty comics
move in

Poor old Martyn Lewis. The BBC newsreader started a campaign for more good news to be injected into news bulletins but his colleagues gave him pretty short shrift.

The *Sunday Telegraph* called this:

St Martyn's gospel

Even the landed gentry were on their uppers and the pro-liferation of car boot sales at the big country estates was a phenomenon which the *Sunday Telegraph* wrote about under:

Throwing open the stately boot

The announcement of the IRA ceasefire brought acres of coverage and hundreds of headlines but nothing was quite as potent as the quote from a young Irish boy, used in a *Daily Mirror* headline:

I don't know what peace is but my ma says it's a good thing

Some astonishing salaries are paid to top secretaries, the *Daily Mirror* revealed. In a feature about the biggest earners it said that the secretary to TV host Oprah Winfrey had just resigned her £750,000 a year job because she couldn't take the pressure any longer. These people, said the headline, were:

Ruled by their secs lives

After £3,000 in driving lessons and twelve failures, Cambridge don Nicholas O'Shaughnessy finally passed his driving test. It had been, said the *Daily Mail*:

The learning curve

☆

Coverage of the royal family had always been polite and dutiful until the new generation of royals started to live their lives more openly. The floodgates were breached once and for all with the romance between Prince Charles and Lady Diana Spencer. Here was a modern royal love affair and the traditional etiquette was thrown to the winds.

On 16 November 1980, the *Sunday Mirror* claimed to have discovered a secret assignation between Lady Diana Spencer and Prince Charles – on a train in secluded sidings in Wiltshire.

Charles and Diana special royal love train secret meeting in the sidings

☆

Despite great pressure and furious denials from Buckingham Palace, editor Robert Edwards refused to publish an apology for the story.

From then on the newspapers declared open season on the affairs of the royal family.

The *People* ran a story about cost-cutting and thrift at the Palace.

They're guarding the change at Buckingham Palace

☆

When Prince Charles linked up with the SAS for some wild and woolly exercises the *Daily Mail* was swift with:

Special Heir Service

☆

There was much consternation in Britain about the Princess of Wales's decision to bow the knee to the Japanese Emperor Akihito. The Scottish *Daily Record* called it:

Japan-knees

The *Sunday Times* called it:

The Veneration Game

☆

Prince Charles showed his courage climbing to the top of the Avon suspension bridge, even with the aid of a safety harness. The *Bristol Evening Post* said:

It's his Royal Harness

☆

Problems with your partner snoring? Apparently Prince Charles has the solution and it was explained to us by the *Sun* in a banner headline:

Charles: why I stick toothpaste up my nose

Less complimentary was *Today* when the Prince was faced with giving the kiss of life to a dummy. 'I've not done this for a bit. One needs practice,' he said offering himself up for ridicule. The paper obliged with:

A thousand years of breathing has gone into this

Princess Diana's appearance at a New York charity function with her hair slicked back caused a sensation – but then one suspects a change of nail varnish by her would still get headlines. On this occasion the *Liverpool Echo* announced wittily:

Hair Oil Highness

The Queen's reference to her 'annus horribilis' may have caught non-Latin scholars by surprise but the *Sun*, in its inimitable fashion, gave us the translation:

One's Bum Year

It was revealed that the taxpayer was funding 217 royal palaces and paying for royal retainers' grace and favour accommodation. The bill, being picked up by the Department of National Heritage, was a staggering £20 million a year. The *Daily Mirror* called it:

£20m disgrace and favour

☆

Some weeks later *Today* had the same idea – or at least found the same inspiration – with a feature about the lavishly decorated homes the Queen rents out to friends and retainers for very modest sums of money:

Disgrace and favour

☆

But Her Majesty reacted to obvious public concern about the cost to the public of re-building Windsor Castle by throwing Buckingham Palace open for £8 a time tours.

The *Sun* told readers that after 231 years Buck House was open to the public and headlined the story cheekily:

Not in here
I'm on the throne

☆

Royals on holiday in Spain were apparently swimming through some of the filthiest waters on the Med. Reporters described how the young Princes were seen ploughing through murky slicks of sewage. *Today* told us:

The drain in Spain falls
mainly on those who reign

Princess Diana's frequent jaunts to sun spots attract a plethora of papparazzi just waiting for that bikini shot. Lounging on King Juan Carlos's yacht off Majorca she was pictured in a tiny red bikini – a picture which was accompanied in the *Sun* by the headline:

Itsy bitsy, teeny weeny,
Di's a dream in her bikini

It wasn't just Princess Diana who was photographed in private moments. A German magazine got hold of photos of Prince Charles naked as he dressed in his bedroom in a French chateau. The British newspapers sensibly declined to use the pictures but it didn't stop them writing the story. The *Daily Mirror* said:

Wunderbare! Frauleins are going
barmy over Charlie's salami

On a visit to Sunderland the Prince of Wales, who has been presented with the most bizarre things on his world-wide travels – and dutifully eaten some of them – was shown a box of live maggots. In all honesty this probably didn't come as a shock to the angling royal but for the *Sunderland Echo*'s enterprising journalists it did provide an angle:

The Prince and the pupa!

Notice how often that exclamation mark arrives at the end of a headline. What is its function? To emphasise, and occasionally to add an extra bit of force to a headline which hasn't quite made its point.

A big society wedding attended by a fanfare of royals brought extra security to Uppingham in Leicestershire. The trouble was no one had warned the locals and resident Derrick Gibbs ignored temporary no-parking bollards only to find himself locked up. The *Sun* knew what it thought of the arrest. It bellowed:

A load of bollards

And the *Sun* later told readers that following the royal pair's separation Charles might never have a Queen by his side. It headlined the story:

Throne alone

A royal flexible friend was launched by Prince Charles. For every £100 spent on the credit card, charity would get

25p. The *Daily Mirror* said:

That'll do princely

When Prince Charles was invited on a painting trip to Egypt, he took with him an official artist. The *Daily Mirror* told readers that for the first time he had appointed a woman – 'a stunning, mini-skirted blonde'. Its headline was:

Charles art-throb

Former Manchester United star striker Bobby Charlton went to Buckingham Palace for his knighthood and the *Daily Express* memorably summed the moment up with:

He's the man
you knighted Ma'am

Rich and famous guests at a charity ball were invited by prankster Jeremy Beadle to drop their trousers to raise extra funds. Guest-of-honour the Duchess of York was pictured surrounded by men with their trousers at half mast. The *Sun*'s headline was:

Waiter, waiter!
There are flies in one's soup

5

Politics

'There are some politicians who, if their constituents were cannibals, would promise them missionaries for dinner.'

H. L. Menken

The *Sun* has led a vitriolic campaign against the bureaucrats of Brussels. The ecu came in for special treatment and it invited readers: 'At midday tomorrow *Sun* readers are urged to tell the French fool where to stuff his ecu.'

It told the EU president Jacques Delors on behalf of its readers:

Up yours, Delors

☆

And later it took great pleasure in Margaret Thatcher's denouncement of the Delors plans for a federal Europe.

Maggie Savages Jacques The Ripper

☆

Delors' replacement was no more popular. When Norman Tebbit laid into the latest piece of Euro-legislation from Jacques Santer, the *Sun* announced:

We Don't Believe
in Santer Clause

☆

And much later when the fish wars broke out Prime Minister John Major gave Spain's man in Brussels, one Mr Elorza, a stern ticking off. This, off course, was irresistible for the *Sun* which recycled the old headline once again:

Up yours, Elorz

☆

But it wasn't just national newspapers which expressed scepticism about Europe. When local MP James Moorhouse called for the right to reject European Commissioners, the *Epsom and Ewell Herald* headlined the story:

Vague in Spain
fell mainly in the disdain

☆

When the time came for Denmark to vote on Maastricht, journalists discovered an amazing thing. The voters there understood! They knew the issues and they knew what they felt about them. They were, said the *Guardian*:

Small and perfectly informed

☆

Still in Denmark, voters were somewhat disillusioned with their political leaders and voted-in a comedian at their general election. His promises included more presents from Father Christmas. Orthodox political leaders like Uffe Elleman-Jensen were a little dismayed. The *Financial Times* called it:

Huffy Uffe

☆

Kenneth Clarke's plan to sell off part of the Treasury to property developers in return for a newly refurbished building by the year 2001, was greeted in *The Times* thus:

Clarke's 2001 space odyssey

☆

When John Major vowed to stop the 'pay and perks bonanza' of Britain's privatised industry bosses, some expressed scepticism. The *Daily Star* announced bluntly:

Fat's Yer Lot

☆

Guardian columnist Suzanne Moore said that she had nothing against people being paid what they were worth, it was just that nurses and midwives, for instance, never were. Why was it always the bosses. The headline summed her piece up cleverly:

Angels with dirty bosses

☆

It soon emerged that the Greenbury Committee, set up to examine the excesses of privatised monopoly bosses, would not be recommending any new laws to stop them. *Today* announced:

Escape claws
for fat cats

☆

Later, *Today* reported that an angry and frustrated John Major admitted that he could do little to stop the share options and bonus-payment perks of the bosses. The newspaper told readers of his admission under this headline:

Fat cats
have me licked

☆

It wasn't only the privatised bosses who were getting the perks, it seems. *Today* said that more than 1,000 civil servants leaving Hong Kong before the Chinese take over the colony in 1997 have been told that instead of a swift flight home they can cruise home on the QE2 in luxury. The cost to the taxpayer, it announced, would be over £13 million. The headline was:

Sir Humphreys
go on £13 million cruise

☆

Government appointed, unelected, administrative bodies in Wales came in for strong criticism in a *Guardian* article under the headline:

The last quango in Powys

It was a headline which re-appeared six months later in the marketing magazine *Adline*, demonstrating that a good headline has mileage beyond measure.

☆

Green councillor Roger Winter was eagerly sought by the Highland Regional Council after leaving it with unpaid fax bills and without the return of an expensive computer. The *Nairnshire Telegraph* summed up the whole affair with this headline:

Where is the
Winter of their discontent

☆

The developing passion for nuclear devices in the Far East was causing deep concern to western nations and produced a lengthy investigation in the *Economist* which headlined its story:

Dedicated followers
of fission

Curiously enough that same headline re-appeared over a similar story in the Communist newspaper the *Morning Star*.

This must have been a coincidence. We can't imagine that the arch opponents of a free market would borrow a cup of sugar never mind a headline from a magazine which believes in the complete opposite.

The new president of South Korea, Kim Young Sam came to Britain for a two-day visit, primarily to set up a consortium which would supply light-water nuclear technology to North Korea. The *Guardian* suggested that this might be:

Fission trip
for Kim

John Major's love of cricket and cricket commentary has long been used against him in headlines. For those who recalled the classic commentary blunder from an England versus West Indies test: 'The batsman's Holding, the bowler's Willey' this *Scotland on Sunday* headline will have extra resonance:

The country's folding, the batsman's Major

☆

House of Commons speaker Betty Boothroyd, tired of the bar-room atmosphere of Prime Minister's question time, told MPs that in future question time would be restricted to questions and answers.

The *Herald* in Glasgow announced without any apologies to Bob Dylan.

The answer, my friends, to MPs bellowing in the wind

☆

MP John Browne was attacked in the press after it was revealed that he had broken Commons rules which prevent MPs exploiting their powerful position. The *Sun* likened him to Rik Mayall's creation Alan B'Stard in the TV series.

A right B'Stard

☆

Angry Scottish farmers were outraged by new moves which they believed would hit their crop incomes. The *East Lothian Courier* summed it all up:

Farmers accuse
Scottish Office
of cereal killings

Scotland on Sunday's analysis of Kenneth Clarke's second budget was headlined simply:

Clarke's budget:
the applause and effects

The confession by Liberal Democrat leader Paddy Ashdown that he had a fling with his secretary gave the *Sun* the opportunity to immortalise him as:

It's Paddy Pantsdown

And it claimed to have helped win the election for John Major with its campaign to persuade readers to vote Tory – a campaign which climaxed on election day with this headline:

If Kinnock wins today will the last person to leave Britain please turn out the lights

☆

Within six months, however, the *Sun* was attacking John Major for a series of political disasters. One of many dark days was the ERM crisis which saw interest rates rocket. It announced:

Now we've ALL been screwed by the cabinet

☆

And, within a month, on an otherwise blank front page:

This page is dedicated to Michael Heseltine. It represents all that he understands about the worries and fears of the ordinary working people in depression-hit Britain. Nothing. Absolutely nothing

Australian prime minister Paul Keating became known for the ripeness of his language and the *Sunday Times*, in a profile, left us in no doubt about it:

Stupid foul-mouthed grub piece of criminal garbage pig sleazebag dimwit sucker perfumed gigolo harlot boxhead alley cat barnyard bully thug clown stunned mullet rustbucket pansy hare-brained hillbilly nong vermin dullard clot corporate crook dummy mangy maggot pissant loop half-baked crim gutless spiv champion liar bunyip aristocrat cheat scumbag fraud ninny fop dimwit liberal muck . . .

It's probably the longest headline in history and the irony is that this was only a fraction of the invective heaped by Keating on his hapless opponents over the years.

A little later he managed to upset both the conservationists and industry with his decision on Tasmania's forests and the *Mercury* there dubbed him:

Forest grump

The ability of former ministers to get themselves lucrative jobs after leaving government is no modern phenomenon, but the latest outbreak of criticism probably started after former Chancellor Nigel Lawson quit the cabinet and took a clutch of well-paid directorships. The *Sun* was quick to lambast him:

One Lawson for the rich

☆

His successor Norman Lamont had it no better from the *Sun*. After a budget which hit virtually everyone in the country – described as a £17 billion tax hike – he was compared with the screen horror Freddie Kruger in the headline:

Nightmare on
Norm Street

☆

For some while after that Lamont stoutly claimed that he could see green shoots, buds of May, a light at the end of the tunnel, etc. as the economy staggered along weakly. It is the lot of a Chancellor to try to talk up the economy. On 15 April 1993 he spoke to the *Guardian* and his claim was headlined:

Future is bright

☆

It didn't seem so and the economy failed to respond. A few

weeks later, on 27 May, the embattled Chancellor was interviewed once again in the *Guardian* and his ironic quote was used as the headline:

I am sure that I seem responsible for the sinking of the Titanic

Not that, perhaps, but probably everything else so far as John Major was concerned because, with immaculate timing, only a day later the *Guardian* headline read:

Humiliated Lamont makes a grudging exit from the cabinet

The internal strife among leading Conservatives had reached fever pitch and former government colleagues Tristan Garel Jones, the minister for Europe, and Edward Leigh, the trade minister, were seen attacking each other in various newspapers. The *Sunday Telegraph* said:

Fury stalks the corridors of glower

The new chancellor, Kenneth Clarke, strolled into the Treasury all smiles and wisecracks. What was life going to be like under Clarke? The *Guardian* offered:

A guide to life under
KC and the Sunshine Band

☆

Not long after, John Major's problems were apparently behind him, according to some experts. He was now going to leave clear water between him and the Labour Party. That view didn't impress some – especially the *Hartlepool Mail* which wrote a column expressing scepticism about his chances. The headline writer caught the theme by recalling a rock and roll band of recent years:

Little credence in
'clearwater' revival

☆

Regeneration was a theme in the *Finchley Advertiser* which reported a public meeting held to discuss the rebuilding of the borough's run-down areas.

Talkin' 'bout
regeneration

☆

Remember *glasnost* and *perestroika* – that brief era of apparent stability in Russia pioneered by President

Gorbachev? A *Sun* cameraman captured the president feeding nuts to squirrels in the garden of his dacha outside Moscow under the headline:

Glasnuts

Power is an infuriatingly transient thing and lasts only as long as the job, as Gorbachev discovered. President Clinton was just getting used to the trappings and kept his plane, Air Force One, standing on the runway at Los Angeles airport while he had a $200 haircut. His opponents were apoplectic. The *Guardian* said:

Scissors out over
Hair Force One

MP David Mellor was merely one of a string of Tory politicians who resigned after admitting having affairs. His, admittedly, was one of the more colourful, thanks to the lurid description of his love-making which apparently included bouts of toe-sucking. His departure was hailed in the *Sun* as:

Toe job to no job

Some years later, when *Sun* editor Kelvin Mackenzie left the newspaper to take up a career in satellite television, the

Guardian, cheekily, combined various famous Kelvinisms to produce this headline:

Gonna: Mackenzie slips
from Sun job to sat job

There was a steady stream of politicians resigning in similar, if less dramatic, circumstances to those of David Mellor. But everyone seemed baffled by the decision of public service minister Robert Hughes to resign. No one knew about his affair until he revealed it. The *Daily Mail* declared:

'Fall of the Pinner Sinner'

The *Daily Mirror* was even more censorious:

Another one bites the lust

Prime Minister Thatcher, dining with colleagues, ordered steak and kidney pie. 'And the vegetables?' asked the waiter. 'Oh, they'll have the same as me.' The story comes from a book of anecdotes reviewed in the *Kentish Times* under:

Maggie shoots from the quip

☆

The GATT talks are unpromising material for headline writers crammed as they are with talk of tariffs and mechanised plantations. But when a row broke out with Latin American countries over the $2.7 billion banana market, the *Financial Times* headline writer saw his chance:

Move to mend
banana split

☆

The East London People's Alliance, a newly formed grouping of disaffected Labour Party members, captured a prize scalp with the defection to it from Labour of veteran councillor Ted Johns. This hot political news was brought to readers of the *East London Advertiser* under the headline:

God ELPSA – Ted quits
East End Labour group
for new party . . .

☆

The Department of Transport decided to take legal action against protesters who had delayed road-building at Twyford Down. Only one problem really – what were their names? The boards they carried only had names of wildlife which they claimed would die. Said the *Guardian*: 'The authorities with nothing else to go on are seeking injunctions in the name of fish, butterflies and birds'. The headline read:

Wanted for hindering
road-building on Twyford Down:
Mr Reed Warbler

Tam Dalyell regretted reacting spontaneously to a telephone call from the *Today* programme on the constitutional debate. Especially, he wrote in the *Scotsman*, since it took place in a telephone kiosk 'when the door will not shut properly in a howling gale, stinking of urine, outside a village pub . . .' The lesson, explained the *Scotsman* headline, was simple:

Soundbitten, twice shy.

When watchdogs threatened a clampdown on electricity prices, shares plummeted. The one million people who bought Powergen and National Power shares were therefore ripped off, the *Daily Mirror* told readers, announcing:

Watt a rip-off

☆

The local government shake-up over unitary authorities was causing severe political ructions in Christchurch. The *Evening Echo* in Bournemouth reported the former Mayor's complaint that the town was 'being sold down two rivers' with the headline:

It will all end
in tiers

☆

The recovery of the British economy was like the first cuckoo of spring – many claimed they had heard it but where was the proof? The *Guardian* examined the continuing claims with the headline:

Darling buds
of maybe

☆

Sex scandals in high places rumbled on throughout most of 1994 and 1995. Hardly had one died down than another appeared and so it was with the so-called 'Bonk of England' saga. Mr Pennant Rea had barely left the bank in disgrace before the newspapers were claiming naughty goings on in the foreign office. The *Sunday Mirror* captured it neatly with:

First the Bonk of England
now the Fornicating Office

☆

Democracy may have come to many former Iron Curtain countries but in some the gun was more popular than any material benefits which might ensue. Not like us, said the *Guardian* with the headline:

Britains never, never will be Slavs

☆

The row over fishing rights between Spain, Canada and Britain seemed to unite Canada and Britain against our EU partners. The highly prized Newfoundland turbot was the source of the dispute and for the *Independent* it meant:

Support for the Canadians is turbot–charged

☆

The *News of the World* had probed the scandal and found the man they claimed was responsible for Spanish fishermen breaking EU rules. He was, of course:

The Codfather

☆

The Times, rather unusually, went hook, line and sinker for the pun and told readers:

MPs flounder wildly as Commons codswallop trawls the depths

And similarly, after a row in the Commons, the *Daily Mail* announced:

Fish minister gets a battering

☆

After some sophisticated mathematics, Education Secretary Gillian Shephard announced a 2.7 per cent pay award for teachers – but left it unclear who might end up footing the bill. The *Independent* announced:

Shephard's pi and other costly sums

☆

The local American airbase at Woodbridge in Suffolk was being sold off to the Maharishi Foundation – a group whose belief in meditation and whose claims of 'yogic flying' have given it an exotic reputation. Local MP John Gummer is a devout Christian and somewhat uncomfortable with the deal but, said the *Guardian*, he had accepted its sale to the highest bidder.

Gummer hit by Yogi bugbear

☆

Loony EU rules and regulations have always made good material for newspapers – the straight banana, the regulation chip, etc. The *Guardian* examined all the alleged rules to see which were myths and which were actually true. For instance, was it true that donkeys would only be

allowed on 'blue' beaches in future if they were wearing
nappies, as had been claimed? The headline:

Eurocrats show red card
to donkeys in nappies

☆

The *Sunday Telegraph* also looked at this story and it found
that the myths, while extraordinary, were sometimes not
a patch on the truth. For instance, for hygiene reasons,
Royal Navy cooks are not allowed any longer to stir their
Christmas puddings in the traditional way, with a wooden
oar.

Truth is stranger than myth
as EEC tries to nail the lies

☆

Unfortunately the stories kept coming and a few weeks later
the Brussels bureaucrats decided that Caerphilly cheese
could no longer be made in Caerphilly. It was all to do
with the unpasteurised milk which the cheesemakers were
using. The *Daily Mail* announced:

Brussels tells cheese man:
You can't make Caerphilly
in Caerphilly

Good news came almost immediately, however, when the *Daily Telegraph* reported that ingenuity had solved the problem. A 75 ft length of hose for transporting the milk into the cheese room instead of buckets, was the answer and Caerphilly was back in business. Their headline said:

Where there's a will, there's some whey

☆

Artist Andy Warhol's parents came from Slovakia. But which town? A battle broke out over who could make this claim and the *Guardian* used Warhol's famous saying for its headline:

Furious for 15 minutes

☆

The scientific community was up in arms over the new White Paper on science teaching from the then education secretary William Waldegrave. It was a case, said the *Guardian*, of:

Science friction

☆

One of the world's last Communist heads of government, Fidel Castro, took some hedonistic pleasures on a visit to the wine cellars of Chablis. The *Daily Mail* couldn't resist this headline:

Fine white for a vintage red

☆

Meanwhile in Peru, the president had ordered his estranged wife to be incarcerated in her rooms in the presidential palace after she threatened to stand against him in the coming elections. The locks on the doors were welded by aides. The *Daily Mirror* called it:

Welded bliss

☆

Wherever you looked political columnist Lord Rees Mogg could be found airing his opinions in the newspapers. The *Sunday Telegraph* profiled him under the headline:

The pontiff of pontification

☆

Education chiefs in Bridport spent £20,000 improving catering facilities at a local school to bring an end to the lengthy queues of young diners. The *Bridport News*'s splendid headline on the story was:

Peas without queues

☆

The *Sun* reported that town-hall staff in Liverpool were being given extra time off if they were gay or lesbian. The same perk apparently applied to coloured, disabled or female staff. Only white heterosexual males would miss out. Its typically condemning headline was:

I'm taking a few gays off

☆

The Commons approved a 30 per cent increase in the allowance of MP Bernie Grant due to his failing eyesight. The *Daily Telegraph* called it, very simply:

Bernie grant

☆

'This picture' announced *Today*, 'shows an extremely rare event: Mrs Virginia Bottomley doing the National Health Service a favour.' No doubt about its feelings there but, just to make sure, it headlined the picture of Mrs Bottomley donating blood with:

About time too ... after all, she's taken enough

☆

For *Today* Virginia Bottomley was something of a *bête noir*. Pictured climbing into the basket of a charity hot-air balloon, they said:

Virginia ... full of hot air as usual

Economic theory is fraught with traps. Keynes, Malthus, Hobson, Smith – they all have their admirers but if following one path were the answer to any economy's problems we'd all be rich. William Rees Mogg in *The Times* examined the flaws under a headline which borrowed from former cabinet secretary Lord Armstrong's famous quote:

Being truthful with the economists

An under-seige John Major was photographed planting delphiniums in his Huntingdon constituency as opinion polls rated him the least popular prime minister ever. The *Sunday Telegraph* story was headlined:

Is Major's garden
going to seed

These euphemisms come to the headline writer's aid on political stories where there is often precious little new to say. Later the *Sunday Telegraph*, on the weekend of the FA Cup Final ran a similar story with the headline:

Major needs a goal in extra time

Labour supporters were spluttering over their breakfasts when they read that leader Tony Blair had spoken admiringly about Maggie Thatcher. Admittedly he had only conceded that she was 'a thoroughly determined person' and 'did some good', but it was a shock nevertheless. The *Independent* said:

Blair admits adoration
of the Maggie

Aspiring Labour MP Barbara Follett, wife of millionaire writer Ken Follett, was selected to fight in the Stevenage constituency at the next election. She swiftly bought a home in the town, although it hardly rivalled the couple's other luxury homes in Chelsea and the Côte d'Azur. The *Daily Mail* said:

Barbie buys dream cottage.
But can Ken park the Jag

A furious row blew up over the multi-million pound sale of Winston Churchill's papers. The national lottery fund was giving nearly £13 million to the Churchill family for the papers. Both the *Sun* and the *Daily Mirror*, echoing the wartime leader's most famous speech, said:

Never has so much been paid
by so many to so few

6

Weird and wonderful

'You can only predict things after they've happened.'

Eugene Ionesco

Newspapers are made up of many things but it is the remarkable, the significant and the bizarre which makes them compelling. Editors have to choose from a vast, shifting framework of elements when making their newspapers each day. Some stories run and run, others disappear with the next day's fish and chip wrappers.

This section celebrates the weird and the wonderful – those odd and unpredictable items which provide the seasoning for your newspaper.

Whatever happened to necrotising fasciitis? Do you remember that killer plague which was eating away at people's flesh and which, for a couple of weeks, frightened the life out of most of us. The *Daily Star* memorably headlined its story then:

Killer bug
ate my face

☆

An Irish company had a big success on its hands, doubling its turnover, with a mat on which cows kneel to be milked. 'Cows know a good thing when they feel it,' said Cow Comfort owner Tom Duffy. The *Independent on Sunday* subs also knew a good thing when they heard it. Resisting any obvious headline tricks they recalled their Latin primers:

A moo amas a mat

☆

A quite bizarre story in, where else, the *Guardian* told readers about a Finnish professor's plans to release a CD of Elvis Presley songs in Latin. They would include 'Tenere me ama' ('Love Me Tender') and 'Nunc hic aut numquam' ('It's Now or Never'). And so, the headline read:

Nunc hic aut numquam
for Finland's fans

☆

An American psychic fought, and won, a court battle for custody of a 35,000-year-old warrior spirit, against a German medium who claimed she had exclusive rights to it. The *Daily Telegraph* announced:

Copyright in ghost case passes to the other side

A new scheme to promote the growing pack of new poets was hailed in the *Journal*, Newcastle, with a headline which would have made Wordsworth's heart swell with pride:

We will wander only as a crowd, say poets

For centuries pigs have been used to snuffle out the prized black truffles under oak roots in south-west France. The arrival of a mechanical device to replace the pig was greeted with deep scepticism in the *Evening Standard* which put it to the test, against Vincent the pig. The machine failed miserably. The headline didn't:

And pigs might fly if electronic machines could sniff out truffles

Reviews of *The Road To Welville*, the film about the bizarre Dr Kellogg, were mixed. His fascination with bodily functions was widely deemed to be unsuitable material for a film. The *Irish Times* was in no doubt. It announced:

Hate Your Enemas

Mildew was proving a major problem for Yorkshire gardeners keen that their prize blooms should win at the horticulture show. *Yorkshire on Sunday* told readers:

Grave problems of victor mildew

The bacteria bred in flies, believe it or not, has curative powers. The *Economist* told the story of the medicines being produced from this bacteria with the headline:

The ointment in the fly

We're a nation of pet-lovers so why shouldn't our pets have their own fast-food establishments? *Auto Express* told its readers about this new phenomenon in America with a neat headline:

Yankee poodle candy drive-in

The secretary of the National Council for Civil Liberties, Mr Andrew Puddephat, no doubt has heard many versions of his name and many attempts to make gags out of it. The *Hendon Times*, reporting one of his speeches, lapsed just slightly from the normal brief, that the headline should sum up the story. You can't blame them. It was a cracker.

I thought I saw
A. Puddephat

☆

The première of the English National Ballet's production of *Giselle* in Oldham was an occasion for ballet lovers but less of one for the *Evening Chronicle* which reviewed the production under the curious headline:

Dances well
for a dead girl

☆

The *Kampala Monitor* in Uganda has an unhealthy fascination for bodily functions and frequently carries stories about the bowel movements of readers. This may reflect the problems of keeping food fresh in such a climate, we just don't know, but here's an example of the sort of story it likes to run:

A man who was hosted by his brother-in-law to a heavy feast and plenty of booze ended up in an RC court after soiling his muko's [in-law's] house with a big heap of pupu [human excreta].

The story was headlined:

Loose bowels shame man at in-law's

The *Monitor* caught *UK Press Gazette*'s eye a couple of years ago with an equally striking headline over a story about a group of parishioners who were disturbed at the delay in the appointment of a parish priest.

It announced bluntly:

Christians pissed off

☆

In Uganda, former Reading gas fitter Ronnie Mutebi was being crowned king, or Kabaka. His father, Freddie Mutesa, fled in 1966 when the monarchy was abolished. Said the *Guardian*:

King Ronnie, gas fitter in waiting, prepares to mount Ugandan throne

☆

Still abroad, the move into Indonesia by a company called Gammon Construction gave the magazine *Construction*

International the chance to headline the story:

Big Gammon stake in Indonesia

☆

The arrival of electronic forms of publishing means that we shouldn't neglect headlines from this source. Teletext has even fewer words to play with than newspapers when headlining news stories, but when it reported on soldiers being flown home from Norway with frostbite it rose to the challenge:

Frost in Norway
gets the cold soldier

☆

The humble six-inch telescope is quite sufficient to the task for most astronomers, *New Scientist* announced under the cheeky headline:

Six inches enough for
amateur astronomers

☆

And over at *MacUser*, the magazine devoted to the Apple Macintosh, there was a review of software produced by a company called Hash Inc. under the subversive headline:

Hash to provide smoother joints

☆

It may just be that it is their generation but rock and roll provides sub-editors with the source of many a headline in today's newspapers.

The *Daily Star* reported on a man who likes to take his pet macaw for a drive. The Beatles might have admired:

Baby you can drive Macaw

☆

Great debate has always raged about whether a headline should tell the story – and thus risk the reader not bothering with those finely crafted words – or whether it should only say enough to tease the reader into the story.

The *News of the World*'s great editor Stafford Somerfield claimed that his favourite headline from the newspaper was:

Incident in a watercress bed

And his second favourite was:

The monster stopped for pie and peas

☆

It was curiously abashed when the Jack the Ripper murders hit the East End of London in 1888. The torrent of detail which used to pour into its headlines disappeared, as though little more needed to be said. One headline said:

Another horrible murder
at Whitechapel

And:

Another fiendish murder
in the East End

But generally the *News of the World* used to specialise in headlines which threw in everything but the kitchen sink, as with this classic about the welfare services chief of a major London borough who was a keen naturist. His pretty model wife had an affair with a gentleman of Oriental extraction who worked at the Co-op bacon factory and in his spare time dabbled in hypnotism.

Nudist welfare man's model wife
fell for the Chinese hypnotist
from the Co-op bacon factory

Although they usually liked to have a vicar or a judge in there somewhere as well.

☆

The twenty-fifth anniversary of that climax of hippydom,

Woodstock, saw a much more commercial attempt at a pop festival on the same site. Hippy idealism was out, free enterprise was in, for a while.

The Times investigated the new spirit of Woodstock under the headline:

The banner–strangled stars

☆

Later, as the festival began and thunderstorms drenched the crowd, *The Times* reported that already four weddings had been performed at the site and one death had occurred. The four weddings seemed a touch contrived for the headline which read:

Woodstock opens with
four weddings and a funeral

☆

A study of seaweed flies has revealed why size is important when selecting a mate, said the *Daily Telegraph*. Apparently the bigger the male seaweed fly the better chance the larvae have of survival. While this was probably true for other animals, the experts remained tight-lipped on whether it had any relevance for humans. The *Daily Telegraph* headlined the story:

Sex, flies
and videotape

☆

For an article about the French city of Rouen and its romantic affiliations – 'a place of assignations and frustrations' said the *Guardian* – the headline was:

Lovers Rouen

☆

One headline which constantly occurs when the subject is discussed by journalists is the one about an escapee from a mental asylum in America who raped a launderette lady and got away. Allegedly the headline announced:

Nut screws washer and bolts

There is no evidence, however, that the headline ever appeared anywhere.

☆

In June 1983, the *News of the World* claimed that three women had been kidnapped in a UFO near Wolverhampton, under the headline:

Close encounter at the Shamrock cafe

☆

In October 1983, the *News of the World* described strange indentations in the soil at a site in Suffolk. These were said to be from an alien craft but were later identified by Mr

Thurkettle, a Forestry Commission official, as 'depressions made by rabbits'.

The *News of the World*, undeterred, claimed:

UFO lands in Suffolk
– and that's official

A survey of librarians revealed that the top ten impromptu bookmarks used by borrowers was headed by bacon rinds. Others included used condoms, a £20 note and a letter threatening legal action for the theft of library books. The *Guardian* said:

Bacon bookmarks
baffle librarians

Rudyard Kipling's *Just So* stories told us how the elephant got his trunk – its nose was stretched by a crocodile. Had Kipling still been around he would have learned how the elephant is losing his trunk, according to the *Sunday Telegraph* which warned that a disease is causing their trunks to rot:

How the elephant lost his trunk

The Maharishi Foundation, which espouses transcendental meditation and whose higher practitioners claim the skill of 'yogic flying' by the power of meditation, bought the former American airbase (what else?) at Woodbridge in Suffolk.

The *Ipswich Evening Star* announced:

Yogi Air

And possibly even more alarmingly came this news from the *Financial Times*.

Commerzbank agrees to buy Jupiter

Is nowhere in the solar system safe from the German beach towel?

It wasn't, of course, buying the planet so much as a UK-based fund management company. But for a moment there everyone choked on their breakfast toast.

A pot-noodle advertisement which, it was claimed, had caused three people to have epileptic fits was banned by the Independent Television Commission because it used disturbing flashing images. The *Guardian* said:

Flashing TV pot noodle advert banned after epileptic attacks

☆

Both the *Daily Record* and the *Yorkshire Post* carried the extraordinary story of the retired teacher who had his leg amputated in Spain and was told formally to bury it. Donald Warren and his wife Trish thought it might be a joke until the undertaker arrived at the hospital with a selection of caskets. Now his leg has its own little plot complete with plaque. The headline writers chose very different angles.

The *Yorkshire Post* went for the simple:

One foot in the grave

While the *Daily Record* offered the stark:

Leg op Don to rest in pieces

The *Guardian* carried an article about carnivorous plants – potatoes that eat protein, seeds that eat flesh etc.

Meat and two killer veg

Environmental officers at Scarborough council have decided to use an audio distress call to deter troublesome seagulls rather than the cruel stun-bait which they used before. The *Yorkshire Post* reported the story thus:

Big gulls do cry

The company which owned the trademark on Noddy threatened to sue an artist who used him without permission. Said the *Guardian*:

Noddy goes to court as copyright owner plays the part of PC Plod

☆

Two librarians who carried out a long-distance love affair on the Internet and finally married were kept apart by Australian authorities who ruled that Charlene Boot was too fat to come into the country. The *Guardian* reported the strange but true tale under this headline:

It's not over until the fat lady slims

☆

We took this one with a pinch of salt – or should it be monosodium glutomate? According to the *Sun*, a Chinese chef cooked his friend's lottery numbers. Yes, when someone called to tell his friend what lottery numbers he had ticked, chef Steven Lam thought it was a take-away order and rustled up sweet and sour pork, king prawns, crispy beef and other goodies.

The *Sun* headlined this:

National wokkery

☆

And that was no less bizarre than some of the causes which benefited from the national lottery. The Ikon Gallery in Birmingham's Ladywood received £100,000. The *Daily Mail* discovered that it was displaying 500 lb of potatoes connected by wires in an avant garde exhibition. It said:

This week's lottery good cause,
500 lb of artistic potatoes

The Elfin Oak in London's Kensington Gardens is an ancient tree trunk carved with fairy figures by sculptor Ivor Innes in 1911 and a favourite landmark for youngsters. The *Sunday Telegraph* warned that the carvings were now deteriorating and there was no money available for repair, under this headline:

Curse of cuts in spending
falls on fairyland

☆

Spare a thought for this family from Surrey. Some years ago the son sliced the top off his finger in a door only to see a chicken run off with it.

Was it coincidence or something more sinister when last year the father chopped his finger off in a garden accident only to see a duck eat it! The *Horley Mirror* covered the story with the headline:

Duck ate my finger, says dad

☆

The death of Mr Alfred Butts gave some of the more learned newspapers a field day. Not that they rejoiced in his death, far from it, but Mr Butts was the inventor of Scrabble. Said the *Guardian*:

Mr Scrabble runs out of letters

☆

And later in an obituary which explained that he had been a boon to word enthusiasts or logogriphers, enabling them to use words like aureolae, the headline was almost impenetrable:

Aureolae for logogriphers

☆

Religious broadcasting wasn't supposed to be entertaining, complained BBC listeners when Radio One disc jockey Simon Mayo announced his new series called 'The Big Holy One'. Their anger was hardly assuaged when Mayo promised that the series would be 'a revelation'. The *Guardian* headlined the story:

The Big Holy One
takes the Michael out of saints

☆

And when it became legal for religious groups to advertise themselves on television, the *Guardian* asked advertising companies to prepare sample campaigns for the Church. One such company prepared a campaign which included the curious advertisement: 'Why are children mugging grandmothers? God knows.' The *Guardian* headlined its piece:

Ad gloriam

When a fire-worshipping German painter took up ownership of the 7,500-acre Hebridean island of Eigg for a reputed £1.5 million, the suspicious islanders greeted his arrival with apprehension. The *Guardian* announced:

Hardboiled Eigg islanders give the new German laird a cagey welcome

If you have ever had cause to wonder what Robert Louis Stevenson meant in *Treasure Island* when the pirates sang 'Fifteen men on a dead man's chest', then the *Daily Telegraph* finally offered the answer. Dead Man's Chest, it had gleaned from the Royal Geographical Society magazine *Geographical*, is part of the British Virgin Islands. Its headline on the story was:

Solved: 15 men on dead man's chest

A firm of funeral directors was packed out when it held an

open day inviting members of the public to look around.
The *Western Gazette* said:

People dying to get into open day at funeral parlour

What the customers of the funeral parlour wear is due a
change if funeral fashion expert David Holt has his way.
He came to the UK to show off his range of clothes which
would replace the dowdy old shroud. The *Sunday
Telegraph* announced:

From here to eternity in a pink negligee

Can animals go to heaven? The then Archbishop of York
Dr John Hapgood said that experiments upon apes and
other animals were a matter of concern because they could
have souls and go to heaven. The *Daily Telegraph* used a
little play on words with:

Apes may have souls too, says Primate

Russians holiday in Crimean resorts on the Black Sea, the
Daily Mirror told us, because the strong salt content in the

water was therapeutic. It was:

The life of brine

It's not just traffic hold-ups that have a hotline these days. The *Guardian* reported that a daffodil hotline had been set up in the Lake District for Wordsworth admirers to find those golden hosts.

Wordsworth hotline gives details of daffodil movements

A prize-parrot owner was told by his neighbour that the bird had died while in his care and had been buried. The man suspected that it had been sold instead and was demanding that it be dug up. The *Sun* said:

Cock-a-tomb!

Scientists believed they had found the shirt of St Thomas à Becket who was murdered by four knights in Canterbury Cathedral in 1170. A turbulent priest he may have been but he was also enormous. The shirt size suggested at least 6ft 8in tall. The *Sunday Telegraph* said:

Shirt size suggests Becket was a giant

Who makes the best fish fingers? The *Daily Mirror* found that Marks and Spencer only sell German ones but did a test on children to see which they preferred. The result was clear. British ones were best and they told the M&S executives:

Codswallop

A zoo, dubbed 'animal Auschwitz', was the centre of controversy when it was alleged that the keepers sat down to a meal of baby bison. The *Daily Star* told readers about it with this shocking headline:

Zoo men
roasted a bison

A cheeky T-shirt manufacturer was in trouble with the national lottery organisers after using their logo on his latest venture, shirts which announced 'I've won bugger all'. The *Sun* exploited the national lottery slogan to tell the story under this headline:

It could be sue

The arrival of the designer jelly baby caused a momentary stir in the newspapers. Trebor Bassett decided that this age-old confectionery could do with a make-over and dressed them with baseball caps and bumbags. The *Daily*

Mail greeted this with the headline:

Babies with attitude

☆

And jelly babies weren't the only thing getting a face-lift. Unigate Dairies decided that the traditional milkman was due a change of image and re-named theirs 'home delivery salespeople'. *Today* said:

Ernie, the fastest home delivery saleperson in the west

☆

British Rail's problems didn't end with leaves on the line and the wrong kind of snow. Travellers on the Waterloo to Honiton service were re-located when an announcer told them there were fleas in the rear carriages. The *Daily Mirror* said:

Wrong fleas on the line

☆

The spirit of a Canadian airman who hung himself in a York pub returned to frighten the life out of a young woman. It was the second time this ghost had appeared, said the *Yorkshire Evening Press*. A case of:

An inn-spectre calls – again!

Much of eastern England was hit by a foul-smelling wind which worried householders and had the switchboard at gas companies blocked with callers fearing leaks. The smell was eventually traced to pig dung and urine slurry being spread on fields in Holland and carried by freak weather conditions. *Today* said:

Phew!
What a porker

☆

A stray cat wandered onto a greyhound track in the middle of a meeting and used up most of its nine lives. The greyhounds fell over themselves in a chase for the moggie and ignored the hare. The *Daily Star* said:

The cat crept in, trapped
and crept out again

☆

Scientists in America, presumably with nothing better to do, decided to see what happens if you give spiders hallucinatory drugs. Amazingly they discovered that spiders spin their webs in a different way when under the influence. The *Independent* said:

A spot of speed
put spiders in a spin

The *Daily Telegraph* which also covered the story said:

Drug-test spiders
weave their way home

☆

The tabloids caught up a day later with the *Sun* announcing:

A-crack-nophobia

☆

And the *Daily Star* calling them:

Spaced-out
spiders

☆

Global warming has been attributed to many things. We once saw a story in the *The Times*, of all places, which claimed that it was exacerbated by cows farting. So we weren't quite so surprised as most to see the *Guardian* and the *Daily Telegraph* carry a story which claimed it was termite farts which were the problem.

The *Telegraph* announced:

Flatulent termites
cast a cloud over the world

While the *Guardian* said with an apparently straight face:

Flatulent ant
guilty of inflating global
greenhouse gas levels

☆

The *Guardian* reviewed a new biography of Tom Paine by claiming it was far too long and, probably, unnecessary. It was all the fault of computers, said the reviewer, which made writing so easy. The headline announced that this was:

Endless erudite
ejaculation

☆

Foreign language is seldom used in headlines for the obvious reason that most of us still haven't caught onto the notion that there is any other language really worth speaking than our own. But sometimes is it irresistible.

The *European*, who else, showed how well it can be done when it reported on the changing face of Paris's best-known road, the Champs Elysées. It's literary headline was:

A la recherche du Champs perdu

☆

But the classic by which all others are measured was an American newspaper headline about film star Gloria

Swanson and her drink problem:

Sic Transit Gloria Swanson

The *Sunday Times* reviewed a difficult to understand book called *Fuzzy Thinking* by Bart Kosko, with a headline which recalls the words of philosopher René Descartes:

Cogito, ergo . . . um

The original Descartes nostrum was 'cogito, ergo, sum' meaning 'I think, therefore I am'.

Faced with a story about the deep significance of spam to Americans, where the annual Spamarama regularly attracts 2,000 spam lovers, the *Guardian* picked up on the quote from spam devotees' spiritual leader David Arnsberger. 'Spam is the common unconsciousness of the American public,' he said. The headline said:

I'm pink, therefore I'm Spam

In the early years of newspapers, life was tougher and riskier than now and the headlines of the day reflected this fact.

The *Bedford Mercury* of 24 January 1846, reported that Mr William Farrar of Tadcaster died eating beef gravy made with the poisonous root Monk's Hood. It was mistakenly used instead of horse radish. The headline announced:

Death caused by
horse radish

On 14 February 1830, twenty-two agricultural labourers hauled a wagon-load of barley from Daventry to Coventry (twenty-three miles) 'to obtain a trifle towards supporting themselves and their families' reported the *Coventry Mercury*. The next day they hauled coals onwards to Bedworth (ten miles). Its headline said:

Men pull wagons
to support families

The *Carlisle Journal* on 17 February 1824, reported that percussion powder and gunpowder was being placed on wire inside coffins, which would then explode on being opened, to deter an outbreak of body snatching. The headline said:

Foiling the
body snatchers

In April 1805, a boy put a stick, which had been used to catch toads, in his mouth. It is believed that toad venom adhering to the stick, poisoned his mouth producing so much swelling that he died several days later. The *Lancaster Gazette* announced:

Boy killed
by toads

☆

Adams Weekly Courant, 21 December 1773. A farmer tied a cat by its leg to a stake. The cat, perhaps not surprisingly, proceeded to cry, 'and continued doing so for two or three days, and not a crow has been seen.' The headline was:

New way of
scaring crows

☆

The *Gloucester Journal*, 27 December 1762. A man who stole a sheep tied its hind legs together and put them around his kneck to carry it off. When his body was found some days later it was presumed that in its struggle to get away the sheep strangled him. The *Gloucester Journal* reported the story under the bizarre headline:

Strangled
by sheep

7

Sport

'Winning isn't the most important thing. It's the only thing.'

Vince Lombardi

Many editors don't understand sport. They came up through the news or foreign beat, or emerged from the arcane mysteries of the production system. No one ever got to be editor from the sports department. The consequence is that the sports people are often a breed apart – like their headlines.

After a near tragedy during the German Grand Prix, when fuel ignited and the Benetton car was enveloped in a fireball, the horror of the event was captured starkly with the *Sun* headline:

The ignited colours of Benetton

On 30 June 1988, the *Daily Mirror* claimed the dubious honour of putting the word 'arse' in a headline for the first time, over a story about a spat between Australian tennis ace Pat Cash and his rival, the German player Boris Becker. They resisted using the full expletive and said:

You smart arse Kraut

The assault on Nancy Kerrigan and the involvement of her main rival Tonia Harding in the affair opened up the seamier side of international ice-skating – a side of which spectators and fans had been blissfully unaware. The *Sunday Times* described the affair under the headline:

Ice Queen wars bare
skating's dirty underside

And the *Sunday Telegraph*, telepathically, said simply:

Ice Queen wars

Soccer headlines often tend towards the punny rather than the subtle and usually capitalise upon the name of the soccer star who features in the story. Nevertheless, some show a wit and skill which goes beyond the simple pun.

Les Ferdinand's performances for Queens Park Rangers were lauded by manager Ray Wilkins after a performance at the club's Shepherd's Bush ground, and attracted this subtle punning in the *Sun*:

A Ferdinand's
Worth Two in the Bush

☆

And when Ipswich Town were more of a force than they are now, their shock 5–3 defeat by Tottenham and the sending off of Town's striker Eric Gates gave a clever *Sun* headline writer this:

Five bar Gates

☆

England's World Cup performance under manager Graham Taylor may have been slammed by the press, but it's worth remembering that in his time England manager Bobby Robson was treated no better.

Days away from the finals Paul Gascoigne was involved in a clash outside a bar and it was revealed that Robson was already preparing to quit. The *Sun* declared:

World Cup Wallies

☆

England football manager Graham Taylor had a torrid time at the hands of the *Sun* headline writers. First they called him a turnip (it lives in the dark and gets covered in fertiliser). Then they called him an onion after England were beaten by the Spanish.

And as he prepared for the vital qualifying match with

Norway the pressure was telling on him.

'I wonder what vegetable they have in Norway?' he asked reporters fearing the worst from the *Sun*

And that was their headline – along with a summary of his recent record which read:

Swedes ... 2 Turnips ... 1; Spanish ... 1 Onions ... 0

The postscript to all this was, of course, England's defeat by the USA which the *Sun* headlined grimly:

Yanks 2 Planks 0

England's defeat by America at football coincided with the cricket team's defeat by Australia. Everyone, it seemed, was beating the national sides. The *Sunday Telegraph* called it:

That was the week that was when the eagle soared and the kookaburra sang

☆

New England football manager Terry Venables had a long honeymoon period with the press. But he probably knew it wouldn't last and when England slumped to a dull 0–0 draw with Uruguay his moment came. The Uruguay manager called England's players 'brainless'. The *Sun* challeneged Venables:

Prove you're not a turnip, Terry

☆

And when he agreed to make a series of footballing videos – like the one made by Graham Taylor in which the former England manager managed to use the f-word thirty-six times – the *Sun* said:

Oh no!
Terry does a turnip

☆

The England cricket team's performances in Australia had the headline writers screaming with dismay. After Michael Slater plundered his fourth century the *Derby Evening Telegraph* could wait no longer:

England are like
lambs to the Slater

☆

The moment of madness that left Eric Cantona rather worse off and without a game for the rest of the season, had the headline writers in a feeding frenzy. The *Evening Leader* in Wrexham was one of many which came up with headlines on this theme:

Le Twit Hits the Fan

And in similar vein, the *Daily Star* reported on the way that football clubs regularly change their kit to capitalise upon the income from young fans eager to own a first-team replica strip.

When the shirt
hit the fan

Few had any reason to thank Eric Cantona for his extraordinary kung-fu exploits; except, perhaps, Michael Robinson who had just completed his book *La Philosophie de Cantona*. And since he hailed from Northwich, the *Northwich Chronicle* was swift with:

Ooh Ta, Cantona

A very similar headline but on a very different story came from the *Independent on Sunday* which explained that up to 40,000 people were expected at the 'Songs of Praise' TV special from the Manchester United football ground.

Ooh Ah, cantata

And when, after the first hearing, it looked as though Cantona might go to jail, that sensitive lot at the *Sun* announced:

Ooh aah Prisona

Cantona attended a press conference to explain himself but succeeded in confusing us even more with an impenetrable quotation about seagulls and sardines. This was taken to be more of the philosophy of Cantona and the *Daily Telegraph* had a bit of fun with it:

Sardines gutted as Socrates comes in on the rebound

Swimming star Nick Gillingham bought his dream home – a converted barn in the West Midlands – only to have a nightmare with the contractors who went bust leaving endless problems.

The *Sun* told his story under the headline:

My New Home Was A Dive!

The death of Sir Matt Busby was a genuine moment of universal grief in the football world. The *Daily Mirror*'s story about the undertaker's assistant who photographed the corpse and tried to sell pictures warned him that he would be an outcast in the city.

You'll Always Walk Alone

☆

The *Sun* was equally respectful, headlining its account of the tribute to Sir Matt by grieving Manchester United soccer fans:

The Man U Loved

☆

Leeds fans who had disgraced themselves in the previous away match by booing during the minute silence for Sir Matt Busby, went to play Oxford with their reputation in tatters. The *Yorkshire Evening Post* was pleased to report that on this occasion:

Fans pass the Oxford exam

☆

Whitbread Round the World racer Lawrie Smith arrived back in Britain at the end of the third stage after breaking his leg. The *Guardian* announced:

Smith breaks foot in third leg

He didn't break his foot, of course, but they couldn't repeat leg

☆

The battle for the Jules Verne trophy saw Robin Knox Johnson and Peter Blake's *ENZA* cross the finishing line backed by a gale-force wind four hours ahead of the previous record.

The *Guardian* neatly headlined the story:

In flew *ENZA* for world record

☆

A picture special on the Cheltenham Gold Cup in the *Daily Express* was headlined:

Only Falls and horses

☆

Jim Courier's clinical dismissal of arch-rival Pete Sampras from the quarter-finals of the French Open was headlined in *Sports World*:

Signed, sealed, Couriered

☆

Cambridge opening batsman Richard Cake scored an unbeaten 70 on his twenty-first birthday and provided dogged opposition to a strong Lancashire side. The *Daily Telegraph* recorded his performance with this witty headline:

Cake stalls Lancs

There was a certain suspicion about the Coventry Third XV loose-head prop, but it wasn't until half-time that the opposition sussed it. The player was a woman, and the captain's wife to boot. Only eight players had been willing to turn out for the friendly on New Year's Day so Bernadette McFadzean stepped gracefully into the breach after her husband appealed for more players to make up the fifteen needed. The story was reported in the *Yorkshire Post* with the headline:

Excuse me for being a little forward

In a flashback to the final round of the 1972 British Open at Muirfield, the *Scotsman* recounted how Lee Trevino turned to Tony Jacklin and said: 'Nicklaus might catch one of us but he ain't going to catch us both.' He was right, but a breathtaking chip by the Mexican robbed Jacklin of the top prize. The *Scotsman*'s frenetic headline went:

Tex-Mex's true grit hexes vexed Brit

Whether it's the FA Cup or the Stratford Hotel and Caterers' Association Shield Cup Final, the passion is the same and the headline writers are as keen to capture the moment. And when The Wedgnock Inn side, nicknamed Knocker by their supporters, scored two cracking goals in the closing minutes to cruise to victory, the *Stratford*

Herald headline writers knew their duty:

A great pair for Knocker

☆

When former England boss Graham Taylor turned down an offer from the BBC to commentate on the 1994 World Cup in America, the *Liverpool Echo* summed it all up:

Thanks But No Yanks

☆

Boxer Michael Moorer's victory over Evander Holyfield seemed to doom Lennox Lewis to the backwoods, his prospects of a fight for the undisputed title of Heavyweight Champion of the World receding fast. The *Independent on Sunday* summed up the affair thus:

Moorer less for Lewis

Angry Raith Rovers were suspended by the Scottish Football Association after striker John McStay failed to appear for a disciplinary hearing. The *North-West Evening Mail* neatly captured the moment with:

The gripes of Raith

Ross County clinched promotion against Alloa Athletic after scoring two goals and seeing Alloa players Neil

Bennett and Willy Newbigging sent off. *Scotland on Sunday* told readers:

Alloa and goodbye as County rule promotion clash

It was a simple, obvious statement but when it had taken the Arsenal player ninety-eight games over two years, four months, two weeks and two days, the headline in the *News of the World* required little but this:

Jensen Scores

When the Reverend Peter Plunkett vowed to run a marathon to raise money for charity, the *Liverpool Echo* pictured him in flowing cassock over the headline:

You can't get quicker than a quick, fit vicar

Reading Football Club's match-day programme was optimistic about its team's chances of promotion and said so in no uncertain terms:

Bets Still On For Rovers' Return

Newcastle United were less than happy after Tottenham's Teddy Sheringham scored three goals to beat them in a Premier League match. Their feelings wouldn't have improved after the *Sunderland Echo* headlined the story wittily:

Triple Sheri leaves United feeling sick

And the *Echo* came up trumps again after the Reading goalkeeper Shaka Hislop (yes, that's right) kept the Sunderland strikers frustratingly at bay at Roker Park.

Shaka Can – Roker Can't

25,000 soccer fans from Merseyside, without a ticket for the FA Cup Final between Liverpool and Everton in 1986, swarmed into London in the hope of seeing the match. The *Sun* announced:

Sweet FA for 25,000 fans

The message reputedly sent to Arsenal's Anders Limpar by Perry Groves, who stepped in for the striker when he was drafted into the Swedish camp for an international against Germany, was curt. The *Sun* told us it was this:

Stick It Up Your Limpar

The Fulham Football Club magazine appealed for plumbers to help refurbish the players' shower room. Presumably in an attempt to talk to them in the language of the terraces, they headlined the story:

Get your tools out for the lads

☆

The Glasgow Rangers goalkeeper performed heroics to keep his team in the game and, given his name, and the raging controversy at the time about the manner of Captain Bob's death, the headline fell neatly into place:

Maxwell goes down
and Rangers stay afloat

☆

Looking back, it may have been the decision which condemned the England cricket team to such a bad tour of Australia in 1994. The team chaplain was brusquely cast aside by the new regime and the players' spiritual side sadly neglected on that gruelling tour.

The *Evening Standard* summed up the story:

New reign stops pray
for England test team

☆

It wasn't a heroic test series as we all know. The headlines here at home made gruesome reading. They were no better in Australia. Here's what the *Mercury* in Tasmania made of one, especially weak, England performance:

In their bungle, the lion squeaks tonight

☆

The 1995 £21 million Australian bid for the America's Cup – the top prize in ocean sailing – collapsed when the hull of *OneAustralia* snapped, dumping the seventeen-man crew in the sea off California. *Today*, with a lack of sympathy perhaps predictable after England's cricket and rugby league defeats, announced:

Back to the drawing board then, eh, lads

☆

The unexpected win by West Ham at Arsenal was masterminded by their striker Don Hutchison who scored the winning goal. And in the time-honoured fashion of the sports pages he thus had his name immortalised in a headline. The *Sun* bellowed:

Don up like a kipper

☆

The word 'arse' still isn't common currency in headlines but sometimes it just seems to be unavoidable. Arsenal's disaffected striker dropped his shorts after being substituted, offering a revealing sight to spectators. The *Sun* announced:

Wright makes an
arse of himself

☆

Betting ace Graham Hill plotted his coup for years, spending ten hours a week studying sporting odds and tapping them into his computer. He finally came up trumps, winning £813,000 by betting on a golf tournament.

The *Sun* told the story under the headline:

I'd plotted
my hole in one for years

☆

Soccer player Nick Loughlin was sent off for using the word 'bollocks'. He was later given a three-match ban and fined £16. But Nick wasn't taking this lying down, he looked up the word in the dictionary and passed the definition to the FA officials who then cut his ban to two games and the fine to £10.

The *Daily Mirror* used Nick's definition in its clever headline:

An expression of disbelief
to you, ref!

. . . and just in case readers didn't understand, they carried a second headline which said:

Player proves b*****ks is not a swear word

All of which makes you wonder why the *Daily Mirror* was so coy about using the full word.

Legendary rowing coach Dan Topolski was brought in by the Oxford boat race team to help revive their fortunes after some poor recent performances. The *Oxford Times* reported the story under the headline:

We're desperate, Dan

Not much doubt about the success of German footballer Jürgen Klinsmann in fitting into the English game with Tottenham. His goalscoring, his gentlemanly conduct and his apparent humility endeared him to fans and headline writers alike. After he scored two goals in the FA Cup match against Sunderland, the *Sun* headlined its story:

And now Jürgen-a believe us

His name cropped up repeatedly in headlines over his first

few months in the English game. After one fantastic performance the *Daily Mirror* said:

You can search the land and never match Mr Klinvincible

And even later, after he hit two goals in a victory against Ipswich Town:

Jurgenaut

The news that he was being offered a £5,000 a week pay rise to stay with Spurs suggested there might be plenty more to come. The *Daily Star* called him:

Jurgen quidsman

And then the *Daily Star* announced that he could be on his way back to Germany in a big-money transfer. Was this, then, the end of the Jurgenisms?

Jurgen to miss me!

Manager Simon Stainrod's Ayr put in a convincing

performance in beating Dundee, a performance which *Scotland on Sunday* hailed with the headline:

Stainrod's Ayr and graces dominate Dundee

☆

Southampton striker Matthew le Tissier was the idol of every fan at the Dell, their south-coast ground. His performances during the season were outstanding and none more so than in the 6–0 thrashing of Luton. The *Daily Mirror* summed the game up thus:

Del boys 6, Plonkers 0

☆

A volley of bleak headlines screamed out at us after the disgrace of Lansdowne Road. It had seemed that soccer hooliganism was under control, but the England versus Ireland match, called off barely twenty minutes into the game after the outbreak of fascist violence, proved us all wrong.

The *Daily Telegraph* summed it all up with this headline:

The National Affront

☆

The *Scotsman* was keen to get a word with one of Aberdeen's star players, Adrian Sprott, for an article previewing the clash with Stenhousemuir. But Sprott proved doggedly difficult to track down. They managed it, just, and headlined their story:

Wacky world of Sprott

☆

Scotland's rugby performances took everyone by surprise last season. Their win over the French at Parc des Princes was the catalyst for a storming season led, of course, by the indomitable Gavin Hastings. *Scotland on Sunday* reported the Scotland versus France game under the headline:

Hastings' Parc de Triomphe

☆

Some victories are just so overpowering that the headline writers are lost for superlatives – usually having used them all up on lesser glories. When Manchester United thrashed Ipswich Town by the margin of 9–0, there seemed to be a shortage of words on the back pages to describe the scale of their success. The *News of the World*, which uses superlatives week in week out with gay abandon, resorted to another device:

U-Nine-Ted

☆

Paul Gascoigne's weight problem was second only to his injury problems, but in the early spring of 1995 he appeared to be a new man. Weighing in 44 lb lighter, he claimed he was fit and ready to return to England duty and for the *Daily Mirror* this was:

Absolutely flabu-less

☆

North London football club Wealdstone signed an 83-year-old player. It was more of a protest than a football decision since a cash crisis was staring them starkly in the face and they wanted to move leagues. The *Daily Telegraph* said:

Wealdstone put age
before booty

☆

Andy Cole's £7 million move from Newcastle to Manchester United broke all records, but he was having trouble breaking into the England team. The *Sun* chanted:

Oh dear what a Cole-amity,
Tel's flushed Andy
right down the lavatory

Schoolboys down the ages have prized highly the strip of the soccer club which they support. Once that strip changed only when there was an away clash of colours. Nowadays it changes regularly and the suspicion is that this is to extract more cash from the youngsters through the club shop.

When Hunter Davies broadcast an indictment of Manchester United over this, together with many other criticisms, the *Guardian* called it:

Merchandise United

Less condemning was the *Daily Mirror* which reported the staggering £25 million earnings of the souvenir business at Manchester United under this headline:

Gold Trafford

Manchester United couldn't escape the headlines. The FA Cup semi-final replay against Crystal Palace was supposed to demonstrate that both sides could overcome the traumas of the first leg when Eric Cantona was arrested for that kung-fu style kick on a fan.

Sadly it didn't turn out that way. United's Roy Keane was sent off for a disgraceful stamping offence on Palace skipper Gareth Southgate. *Today* said:

They can't stamp it out

While the *Daily Star* said they were:

Back to their old stamping ground

The 'burly-rinas' of Blaydon Rugby Football Club have raised hundreds of pounds by donning tutus and performing their version of *The Nutcracker Suite*. It's not a pretty sight but it goes down a treat in Gateshead, Tyne and Wear. The *Daily Star* called them:

The sugar-scrum fairies

☆

Michael Parkinson, whose column in the *Daily Telegraph* has become a must for many, pondered the problem for elderly and female golfers in lugging a golf bag around. The headline over his piece was:

My wife carries golf balls in her handbag. Is she off her trolley?

☆

Tony Jacklin has someone to carry his clubs – but which clubs? After a poor few years he was experiencing a revival and it was all down to a new set. The *Guardian* said:

A set of Pings, two Pongs and in one bound Jacklin is free

Pings are a make of golf club. A Pong is a 46 inch putter which, according to its makers, is 'for when putting gets a little smelly'.

☆

Still with golf, former world number one Ian Woosnam was waiting to tee off in the pro-am Catalan Open. The *Guardian*'s golfing writer observed how he was left completely alone when his partners Johan Cruyff and Andoni Zubizarreta, the Barcelona manager and goal-keeper, turned up.

Woosnam ignored,
for Cruyff's sake

☆

When groundsmen at the home of Wolverhampton Wanderers found sausages and a Mars bar buried in the pitch they were baffled. It turned out that a family of foxes had been living beneath one of the stands and was in the habit of burying food in the hallowed turf. The *Daily Star* told the story beneath this headline:

Foxes beat wolves –
by a chicken, a Mars bar
and two sausages

☆

Sport should be simple but when money gets involved it becomes extraordinarily complicated. Racing fans cheered Michael Schumacher home to victory in the Argentinian Grand Prix only to discover later that, because he had used the wrong fuel, he was disqualified. *Times* sportswriter Simon Barnes said that too often the pit-lanes of sport were being dominated by Monty Pythonesque rules. The headline on his piece:

Pit-lane Python
open ministry of silly talks

☆

After Norwich City sold their star striker Chris Sutton to Blackburn for £5 million the side lost its goal-scoring touch and plummeted down the Premiership. The *Daily Mirror*, perhaps remembering a John Steinbeck novel, called it:

Canary-woe

☆

In the first leg of the League Cup Final between Arsenal and Sheffield Wednesday, rookie Steve Morrow scored the winning goal. His jubilation was somewhat dampened when he leapt on the shoulder of Arsenal skipper Tony Adams and straight over the other side, severely injuring himself and ensuring that he wouldn't play in the deciding leg. The *Guardian* announced:

Joy today but
sorrow to Morrow

☆

The *Independent* reviewed a much vaunted new film, *Hoop Dreams*, about the pressurised lives of two youngsters in America hoping to become basketball stars.

The promised land
of hoop and glory

☆

Crystal Palace called in a hypnotist to help with preparations for the FA Cup quarter-final clash with Wolverhampton Wanderers. They were apparently to be put into a trance-like state and told to visualise success. The *Sun* headlined its story:

Trances with wolves!

Sadly the match ended in a dull 1–1 draw. The *Sunday Mirror* feared that the hypnotism might have put them to sleep:

Twits in a trance

☆

A cruel blow was dealt to England's hopes of World Cup glory. Subbuteo champion Darren Clark split his fingernail while working in a warehouse. The shock news was delivered to us by *Today*'s headline:

Flick as a parrot!

☆

With so many heavyweight boxing champions around, life

gets very confusing for us. But it's some comfort to know that it's almost as confusing for the managers. Here's Rock Newman, manager of Riddick Bowe, trying to explain who might be called THE champion.

The man who beats the man
who beat the man
who beat the man will be THE man.

Clear now? The *Sun* made it easier with the headline:

300 million dollars
That's the purse for the man
who beats the man who beat
the man who beat the man
who raped the woman

Former Manchester United and England footballer Bryan Robson got off to a storming start as manager of Middlesbrough and the fans at Ayresome Park sensed glory days coming back. The *Daily Mirror* called it:

Awesome Park

8

Editor's choice

'There are just two people entitled to refer to themselves as "we"; one is a newspaper editor and the other is a fellow with a tapeworm.'

Bill Nye

Any selection of headlines is bound to be arbitrary. After all, in an average year something like five million headlines appear in newspapers alone.

So we asked some of the experts, the national newspaper editors, to give us their favourites. Some felt that few headlines worth repeating appeared anywhere outside their own newspaper (well, they have careers to think about) and inevitably some of their choices coincided with ours.

Given the somewhat rapid turnover of editors these days, it will be a miracle if all of them are still *in situ* when this book appears, so please bear with us, and them.

Peter Stothard, editor of *The Times*, was typically generous and selected headlines from a variety of newspapers.

From his own, but before he became editor, was a headline over a story which marked the end of the first year of Boris Yeltsin's traumatic role as President of Russia. The article examined his strengths and weaknesses and with an operatic flourish asked:

Is Boris good enough?

☆

A humorous piece in the late-lamented magazine *Punch* suggested that Beethoven might have written even more fine music had he not been a drinker. The headline was:

Steady on Mr Beethoven, that was your fifth

☆

In 1993 the then *Sun* editor Kelvin Mackenzie went before a parliamentary select committee investigating the role of the press. Far from being on the defensive, his appearance was a *tour de force* which routed his inquisitors. *The Times* headline was:

Kelvin Mackenzie ate my committee

☆

The *Guardian* discovered that archaeologists excavating

ancient remains in Rome had found some questionable building practices. The headline was:

Rome wasn't built in a day, squire

☆

And finally, a headline from the *Sun*. It came after a hefty tax rise during the troubled latter days of Chancellor Lamont and used lateral thinking to make a link between the recurring political sleaze allegations and tax rises:

Now we've all been screwed by the Cabinet

☆

Phil Walker, editor of the *Daily Star*, made his selection from headlines published in his newspaper.

When the valet to Prince Charles spilled the beans on what went on behind the scenes in the Royal household, the heir to the throne was naturally furious.

How mean was my valet!

When an Indian father of three scooped the massive £17 million jackpot in the national lottery:

Vinda loot!

Eric Cantona went missing, it was alleged, when Scotland Yard wanted to interview him in relation to the Crystal Palace affair:

Where aah ooh Cantona?

☆

That new wet look of Princess Diana's, unveiled at an American celebrity night, was dubbed The Flip. The *Daily Star* carried a photograph with the headline:

Di flips her lid

☆

And later:

Hair Oil Highness

☆

One of only five Asian bull elephants in England was killed at a wildlife park owned by Noel Edmonds.

Why the Blobby hell did he have to die?

☆

Not surprisingly, Walker was keen on his Freddie Starr

headline alongside that picture of an apparently aroused Starr in swimming trunks with his new wife.

Is that a hamster in your shorts or are you just glad to see me?

☆

The *Star* used its front page to slam that book written by royal sneak James Hewitt about his relationship with Princess Diana. They urged readers not to buy the book and called it:

A load of old b*!!**ks

☆

The homecoming of Terry Waite was an emotion-charged moment.

They chained up Terry's body for 1,763 days but they couldn't chain his heart

☆

A soccer clash between Wimbledon and West Ham meant a confrontation between two of the toughest players in English football – Vinnie Jones and Julian Dicks.

Dicks 'n' Jones may break your bones

☆

Brian Hitchen, editor of the *Sunday Express*, also chose all his from his own newspaper.

On a feature about a woman who won her boyfriend's love by besieging him with twenty-six red telephone boxes:

Sealed with a loving kiosk

☆

A dog won seven national lottery prizes in a row by picking wooden numbers from the dog bowl with his teeth:

Winalot-tery

☆

Two sisters, who had been separated by their mother's death, met for the first time in fifty-two years at the butchers:

Beef encounter
for long lost sisters

☆

Tunbridge Wells has been immortalised as the town from which 'disgusted' letter writers send their missives to national newspapers. But it can also boast more VCs, ten, than any comparable town.

Courageous of
Tunbridge Wells

☆

It was revealed that Russian scientists were trying to breed a super crime-fighting dog which would have the sense of smell of a coyote.

The hunt for red-hot Rover

Piers Morgan, editor of the *News of the World* selected five of his favourites.

His first appeared above a *News of the World* interview, over tea and biscuits, with Jack 'The Hat' McVitie murderer, Reggie Kray:

I could just murder
another McVitie

The second, also from the *News of the World*, came after it revealed that MP Dennis Skinner, nicknamed 'The Beast of Bolsover' was having an extra-marital affair:

The beast of legover

His third came from the *Sun* after it revealed the extra-marital affair of Liberal Democrat leader Paddy Ashdown:

Paddy Pantsdown

His fourth came on the day of the general election when Neil Kinnock's Labour Party was hopeful of finally bringing down the Conservatives. The *Sun* said:

If Kinnock wins today
will the last person leaving Britain
please turn out the lights

☆

Finally, a memorable headline from the *New York Post* over a grisly murder story:

Headless body
in topless bar

☆

The first headline selected by Sir Nicholas Lloyd, editor of the *Daily Express*, came from his university days when he edited the Oxford University newspaper *Cherwell*. The newspaper published a 'spoof' edition of the local *Oxford Mail* which satirised the way newspapers often seek a 'local angle' from national events:

Oxon man killed
in nuclear holocaust

☆

The open-air concert in Hyde Park by opera singer Luciano

Pavarotti went ahead despite torrential rain. The *Daily Express* headlined its story:

All this for a tenor

☆

A murder attempt on Marks and Spencer boss Lord Sieff failed when the bullet was deflected by his teeth. The *Daily Express* said:

Sieff thanks
his lucky teeth

☆

The *Daily Express* remains one of the Conservative Party's most devout defenders, but it still reports the grim political news – like the failure to hold former Tory bastion Eastleigh in a by-election:

It's beastleigh

☆

And finally, still on the political front, the day after Mrs Thatcher's resignation:

What have they done?

☆

Colin Myler, editor of the *Daily Mirror* is definite. 'My all time favourite,' says Myler, 'was written by Jon Zackon on the *Daily Express*. It was a once-in-a-lifetime story about a saucepan which fell from a kitchen shelf and landed on the head of a parrot perched in its cage below.' The headline read:

Polly put the Dettol on

A *Sun* photographer was the first to show the royal bald patch steadily expanding on the crown of Prince Charles's head. The headline over the picture was:

The heir not so apparent

☆

Myler also liked the headline over a story about frogs who had to cross a main road during the mating season. Many didn't make it. The headline, which took a slight liberty for obvious reasons was:

Halt!
Major toad ahead

☆

Modesty would have stopped him entering this one, which was sent by his managing editor Pat Pilton because it was written by Myler himself. It appeared after the latest Tory politician resigned over extra-marital allegations:

Another one bites the lust

☆

9

Gaffes

'To err is human, but when the eraser wears out ahead of the pencil you're overdoing it.'

J. Jenkins

And finally, some of the ones that went wrong.

Headline writers always used to be told that they needed dirty minds because this would enable them to avoid the embarrassing *double entendres* which can bedevil their craft.

The announcement in the *Cheadle Post and Times* that a married couple were going to entertain the congregation in their local church with a rendition didn't quite get the headline that was intended:

Husband and wife to perform in church

☆

And nor did the departure of Dr Fuchs on his famous Antarctica expedition which was headlined in the *Express and Star*, Wolverhampton, thus:

Doctor Fuchs off to Antarctica

English is a living language and the meaning of words is constantly changing, something which the *Evening Standard* might have taken into account when it headlined a story about political dissent in East Africa:

Jomo stoned at Mboya funeral

What's wrong with the following headlines?

'I'm staying in the street' says Len

Daily Mirror

Drug case Dierdre axed by Co-op

The *Sun*

Hilda Ogden mugged

The Sun

☆

Dierdre and Mike left dancing in the dark

The Times

None of these, of course, are real people. Should headlines in newspapers accord fictional characters the same treatment they do politicians and film stars? And if they should, who's to know when they are talking about real people at all?

The trouble is that viewers seem to regard the characters as real. Ask 'EastEnders' star Todd Carty, whose character Mark Fowler is HIV positive. Sitting down to a meal with his girlfriend, Todd was stunned to hear other diners complaining about him being there for fear they might catch it. Ignorance and stupidity combined, but nevertheless Todd was forced to leave. *Today* said:

Diners hurl Aids taunts at EastEnders star Todd

☆

The *Evening Standard* ran a stop-press piece about the

massive takings over the first weekend of the new Flintstones film.

'Flintstones takes £2.6 million in weekend' it announced. But after a short paragraph came the next stop-press headline . . .

Dozens buried in rubble

This actually related to an earthquake story and someone should have given some thought to a better placement of the two.

☆

Privatisation of British Rail has apparently given some networks more room for enterprise. At least that was what the *Western Mail* was apparently trying to tell us, when its normally excellent spelling record slipped a bit.

Trains freed from yolk

What a yoke!

☆

Even more alarming was the gaffe by the *South London Guardian* reporting a nasty assault near a local tube station.

Woman attacked
by tube station

The mind boggles.

☆

Not while on duty, please. The *Highland News* told readers the story of a drunk who was finally captured by police. Unfortunately this tense drama became a tenses drama.

Police found drunk up on garage roof

Hic!

The nineteenth century photographer John Thomas rightly deserved the retrospective exhibition of his work laid on by the Ruthin and District Association. Sadly, it seemed that something else was on display when the story was published in the *Vale Advertiser*. It announced:

John Thomas on show

Is this a cock-up?

Traffic police launched a new scheme to help lone female drivers should they break down on Greater Manchester's motorways. The *Manchester Evening News* headline didn't quite say what was intended:

Safety code for damsons in distress

The *Liverpool Daily Post* announced that only four weeks away from the opening of the newly merged inner-city hospital, it still didn't have a chief executive. At least, that's what the story said, the headline announced:

Anger as new hospital body
waits for head

☆

During the Falklands War a British hospital ship was heading for Montevideo in Uruguay. The *Daily Telegraph*'s headline, however, suggested something quite different:

Wounded head for Uruguay

☆

The story goes that a headline writer on the *News of the World* was handed a piece about a workman whose pick had cracked a water main showering shoppers. His preferred headline read:

Workman's pick causes flood

But his chief sub-editor feared a misprint on the word pick. 'You're right,' said the man. 'Let's change it to tool.'